To Jean —
a very special
animal Person.
Gary Bo—

It's A Wild Life

.

Gary Bogue

Lesher
Communications, Inc.
Walnut Creek, California

Printed in the United States of America.

Published by Lesher Communications Inc., P.O. Box 5088, Walnut Creek, CA. 94596.

Printed by Dharma Enterprises
1241 21st. Street
Oakland, CA. 94607.

Graphics and Design: Gayle Cornette
Composition and Pasteup: Terri Markey

Photo credits:
Randy Becker, Cover
Jon McNalley, p. 35, p. 55, p. 71
Gary Bogue, p. 3
Eric Rahkonen, p. 87
Mike Macor, p. 103
Bob Pepping, p. 113

Illustrations:
Gayle Cornette, p. 1, p. 69

Columns on the following pages have also appeared in Defenders of Wildlife magazine: 4, 8, 11, 15, 17, 23, 32, 38, 45, 47, 49, 51, 56, 62, 64, 66, 72, 74, 80, 83, 88, 92, 94, 97, 104.

Acknowledgements

Special thanks to:

Deborah Byrd for proofing this book and for being a firm editor; Gayle Cornette for her beautiful layout and artwork; Terri Markey for coding the type and putting it all together so it looks the way it is supposed to look.

The San Francisco Zoological Society Education Department for allowing us to use their tame bobcat Anoki for the cover photograph; Anoki's handler Gail Goodman, who knows her animal well; Tony Bila, assistant head keeper at the S.F. Zoo, for his help and for being Amorak's best friend.

Randy Becker and Jon McNally for proving that it takes a good news photographer to get good animal pictures.

Diane Granados, Operations Manager of the Lindsay Museum, 1901 First Ave., Walnut Creek, for helping us get photographs of Icarus, their non-releasable golden eagle.

CONTENTS

v

Dedication

This book is dedicated to all my foster wild children, and the myriad of hard-working volunteers and veterinarians and special friends who helped rehabilitate them back into the *real* world from whence they came . . .

To Barb, Jeff and Corey who were there through thick and thin . . .

And to a very special mountain lion cub who almost made it, a boy named Sioux.

PART

It's
A
Wild
Life

WILD MAMMALS 1

The Latin proverb, homo homini lupus — man is a wolf to man — is a libel on the wolf, which is a gentle animal with other wolves.
— Geoffrey Gorer, The New York Times Magazine, Nov. 27, 1966

MY WOLF SON taught me a special lesson in life.

Amorak was hurt — and dangerous.

My friend Kim, justly worried, called at noon on a Sunday. (At the San Francisco Zoo, Kim helps give the daily "wolf show." She and several others go into the enclosure, show off the wolves, and give the visitors a lecture on wolves and conservation.)

My associate, Mark Ferrari, and I had obtained Amorak, an arctic wolf, as a cub from a Midwestern zoo so we could raise him and study the predatory development of wolf cubs. The research was completed long ago, and for the last year and a half Amorak had lived in the Wolf Woods Exhibit at the zoo, with Nishka and Kiowa, two northern timber wolves.

Now, something had happened to Amorak's eye, Kim said. It was swollen shut, with bloody fluid seeping out the corners. He was in such pain that he had threatened to attack even those who had worked closely with him for 18 months. And his condition seemed to be getting worse by the minute.

He had been fine on Saturday. But early Sunday morning something seemed to be bothering his right eye. By mid-morning he had chased everyone out of the enclosure. Now it was noon, and he was salivating profusely, periodically arching his head back over his left shoulder in massive spasms, and staggering when he tried to walk.

That morning the keepers had discovered the front of the wolf enclosure was littered with jagged shards of beer bottles.

Kim hadn't phoned just to let me know Amorak was hurt. There was a big problem. The head wolf keeper, the one person in the zoo who might be able to handle Amorak in this situation, was on vacation. Amorak had threatened his assistant. The head veterinarian was also away on vacation, and his assistant couldn't be reached. Nobody with any authority was around to make any decisions — except Kim, a volunteer.

She asked me to come and help — to go into the enclosure, give Amorak a shot to tranquilize him, and help take him to a nearby veterinary clinic for emergency treatment.

I told her to make sure Nishka and Kiowa were locked up in the holding pens. Those two wolves hated me. Enough to kill me, if they could. Mark and I had visited Amorak periodically since he'd been there, and the two were extremely jealous of this relationship — especially Kiowa, who bared her huge canines whenever we came, seared our brains with her penetrating yellow eyes, and dared us to cross the moat.

My wife, Barb, went with me. Mark was out of town (photographing wolves in Alaska, if you can believe it). Barb had been Amorak's foster mother when we'd raised him. There had always been a gentle affection between them — a closeness that even I hadn't shared.

4

And now, after a year, I was going to stroll into the enclosure with a gravely ill Amorak — a possibly confused Amorak who had already threatened to attack people who worked with and loved him longer than I had. And he was going to wag his bushy old tail and let me amble right up and give him a needle in the butt.

Sure he was.

Hey, Mac! It's your old Dad. Remember me? The guy who ran off and deserted you 18 months ago when he left you in a basket on the zoo's doorstep?

Are we still friends?

I pushed my way through the Sunday crowd to the viewpoint above Wolf Woods. It took a minute to locate Amorak — he was lying halfway up the hill about 40 yards away, only his head visible above the grass.

"Hey, Macky," I shouted, unmindful of the stares. "Come on, old boy!"

On any previous visit, that call brought him charging, all tail and wagging body, jaws parted in a massive show of pink tongue and snowy teeth.

He didn't move. Not a muscle. His huge head hung like a great stone carving.

I didn't even exist.

My heart sank. It didn't look good.

Barb wanted to go in with me but after talking it over we finally decided against it. If Mac was as out of it as he appeared, I was going to have enough problems worrying about myself. Terry, one of the regular keepers, said he'd come with me. He could prove to be helpful if Mac tried to take me out.

Nishka and Kiowa started howling their hate at me as we passed the holding cages and entered the display area. It did nothing for one's confidence.

I felt Mac's eyes on me before I saw him, 20 feet away, still lying in the grass. The only thing that had moved was his monstrous head as it swiveled to face me. I saw no recognition at all as his one good eye stared blankly into mine. The other eye was closed and oozing red fluid like sap from a freshly-chopped tree.

As I stood there talking softly to Mac, he suddenly struggled to his feet and stood for a moment, weaving slightly, then staggered slowly toward me. His ears lay back and his eye stared at my face. His tail rose aggressively into the air.

He stood before me, his body as high as my waist, his mouth slightly open, his legs braced apart to keep from falling.

"Hey, Mac," I whispered. "Remember me?"

Slowly his tail lowered and began to wag back and forth and he suddenly reached forward and licked my outstretched hand as his tired jaws parted in a familiar lopsided grin.

I could hear Barb's cry of delight and relief from the other side of the moat.

The trick now was to get him into one of the holding cages where I would have a better chance to knock him out with a shot. Not having the zoo vet's tranquilizer dart gun, I'd have to inject him by hand — something I'm sure Mac wouldn't have let me do even in our friendliest days.

After he finished licking fond remembrances all over my hands (and bringing not a few tears to my eyes) I responded, idiot human that I am, by touching his head.

His yelp of pain instantly silenced the crowd on the other side of the moat. I'd forgotten them. They probably thought or hoped that yelp was from me. I began to feel like some sort of gladiator with the crowd starting to murmur for my blood.

I backed away from Mac instantly at his cry. He wagged his tail in apology, reached out again and took my hand with his mouth and bit down softly to let me know it was all right.

Gently I began to move my hands over his body. Carefully touching a shoulder, his side, his right rump, the long hairs on his chest — looking to find the extent of his problem. Each time his cry of pain jerked my arm. Oh God, was he damaged all over? I turned to Terry, who had a frown on his face. He shrugged back helplessly.

Mac gave us one last look with the good eye and a gentle wag of his tired tail. Then he staggered regally back up the hill to find his smooth spot in the grass. No way were we going to get him down to those holding cages. This was his last stand.

When we regrouped outside the wolf enclosure, we had our first bit of good news. Doc, the zoo vet, had been located and would arrive at any moment. Barb was also there to give me a much-needed hug. My own fears were reflected in her eyes.

Twenty minutes later I stood by watching Doc load the dart gun. We were surrounded by zoo visitors — teen-agers, men, women, mothers, fathers, kids on leashes howling their heads off.

"Hey, you going to shoot the wolf and put him out of his misery?"

"What's he got — rabies?",

"I had a wolf once. They're bad news."

"Gonna kill it?"

"Can I watch?"

Doc really looked tired.

Nishka and Kiowa started howling again when Doc and I entered the enclosure. Nishka threw himself at the bars as we passed by and I shuddered at the hate that made it through.

"They hate me, you know," Doc said sadly. "I've had to dart them and treat them before. The doctor is always the bad guy."

The soft pop of the dart gun was an anticlimax. It happened so fast you could barely see where it hit Mac on the flank, instantly discharging the drug into his body, then fell off into the grass. Mac gave a small hop, looked curiously at his rump and then back at us again. Ten minutes later he was lying on the soft grass and making little puppy running motions with his ponderous paws.

Often when animals are drugged it isn't very pretty. They can convulse and thrash about, fighting the effects of the drug. But Mac was already so weak he just lay down and went to sleep.

Doc pulled his little station wagon into the enclosure through a wooden gate in back. Barb came along and it took all three of us to hoist the wolf's bulk into the back of the car. We were barely able to close the door to hold him in. I sat in the back seat and held his head so he wouldn't be hurt if we hit any bumps.

Half an hour later a group of very relieved people stood around the hospital examining room drinking coffee. There had been a deep cut in Amorak's right eye, probably from a thrown beer bottle. The eye had lost fluid and partially collapsed. But Doc said there was a good chance he'd get back most of his vision. The wolf's extreme pain had probably been caused by some damage to the optic nerve. The pain had been so intense it had affected the actions of his whole body.

Mac was in one of the hospital wards, snoozing off the effects of his tranquilizing drug. The eye had been treated and he'd received an injection of antibiotics. A veterinary ophthalmologist was due in later to check follow-up care.

The wolf, in his weakened condition and extreme pain, had threatened to attack people who had worked affectionately with him on a daily basis for a year and a half, yet he remembered the person who had raised him so long ago from a cub.

And he allowed me, asked me, to help.

How can we continue to allow such intelligent fellow creatures to be killed?

Amorak is fine now. He's back in the enclosure with Nishka and Kiowa, still holding his tail high to mark his position as the alpha wolf in that small pack. There doesn't appear to be anything wrong with his vision.

Speaking of vision, I've gained a little insight myself.

Don't ever lose faith in your friends.

A TALE OF TWO BOBCATS
in their quest for freedom

He was the young city dude, she the shy country lass. Together they made quite a pair.

Our story comes straight from the soap operas. Boy meets girl in strange setting; both locked up together. Only not in jail. In a cage. You see, both our boy and girl are a couple of down-and-out bobcats.

The little male was an old story, one you have heard before. Taken forcibly from his parents while still a baby, he was sold into a life of slavery. He was raised by a nice enough lady who meant him well. But she was, after all, only human. He grew up thinking he was a boy, not a bobcat. You know — be good, love your new mommy, show off for her friends, go in the box, and be sure and lick the blood off your chin when you finish eating your steak.

He never learned how to kill. Never saw a mouse, or knew the freedom of a treetop. He was great on a waterbed, though, and he slept on top of the fridge when the nice lady wasn't looking.

The female came from an old country family. Not terribly refined, but with all the right instincts, plus a heavy-lidded sultriness that more than made up for any small faults she might have had.

I first met the little male last summer. The lady who had owned him — he was about 3 months old the first time I saw him — had tried to raise him in her house like a domestic housecat. This, of course, you do not do with bobcats. Their nutritional requirements are not the same, for example. And "Bobbie" had dietary problems, a calcium deficiency among others. That means he breaks easy if you're not careful.

His owner finally gave him up, but hoped he could somehow be repaired and released back in the wilds. A day late, a dollar short, but he was alive and I had seen worse.

We took him in. With a proper diet, multiple vitamins and a large enclosure where he could bounce and climb and get proper exercise, we could repair the physical damage. But the mental side — that was another story.

Bobbie was tame. He saw himself as "people," and loved to purr and rub against other people's legs.

I recall once having to handle a 6-week-old bobcat kitten that had lost her mama. The kitten, so myopic and blue-eyed she could not see 12 inches in front of her face, was just learning to wobble a straight line. But she nearly shredded my hand off when I tried to pick her up.

Such are wild bobcats. Indomitable and ferocious, and absolute poetry as their fluid, muscular bodies slide through thick brush and up trees in a single bound.

But not our Bobbie. He was content to flop down on top of your foot and purr so hard it loosened the fillings in your teeth.

I had my doubts that this fat, easy going youngster was a candidate for freedom. Better to buy him a car and send him off to prep school so he could grow up and be president.

But that was before we — and Bobbie — met that little country bobcat.

She was a year older than Bobbie, and was another typical story. Struck down in the prime of her young life by a hit-and-run driver, she had been left — a tattered bundle of spotted fur — to die by the side of the road.

One of our animal control officers found her when he was out on patrol. Carefully, he loaded her stunned form into his truck and raced for a nearby veterinarian. After an hour of surgery, in which her shattered left foreleg was fitted with a stainless steel plate, she was transferred to our wildlife center.

I came to work that Monday morning, and Pat — center director, nurse, mother-in-residence — told me to go see the new bobcat.

I did, and nearly did a backward somersault as her snarl and good paw hit the front of the cage at the same time. Sassy cat.

The next morning Pat found her sitting just inside the door to the center, waiting to be let out. She had spent the night chewing through half-inch plywood. She must have gotten ideas from the beaver in the cage across from her.

I suppose it was only natural that the city dandy and the country girl would hit it off.

We had a large outside enclosure, actually two cages in one. We put the little male into the larger section because it housed a tree he could climb in. The smaller side was for her, a place to exercise that bad leg when we took the cast off. To be honest, we were scared to put them together. Him tame and her with a wild temper. I figured she would chew him up into little bits and not even bother to spit them out. So we tried to keep them apart.

But one day a door accidentally slid open, and Bobbie, the little brat, slipped through and ran right up to her and gave her a love bite on the chin. And did she knock his little stubtail clear across the cage?

No, she just purred and snuggled and let him maul and climb over her body and rub and purr in his clumsy teen-age fashion. What else could we do, but leave them together?

Pat and I were delighted. Maybe a bit of her wildness would rub off onto Bobbie and get rid of that infernal tameness. Mainly, I hoped her wildwood wisdom would supplement his lack of smarts.

Last fall we released them. We picked up Bobbie by the scruff of the neck and threw him in a box, and snagged her with a net and sort of did the same.

It took two hours to drive to a place wild enough to free them. There are some very primitive areas in Monterey County, out back of Big Sur.

I could rave about the crimson poison oak with the morning sun shining through it; or the jagged peaks in the distance all gray, then purple, then liquid gold as we came closer; or the little stream we could hear chuckling away at the bottom of the canyon.

But the best part came when Bobbie

walked out of the box first and sniffed his first free breath. She, the wild one, exploded out over the top of him and crashed into the brush and up a nearby pine tree. Confused at first, then with a will, Bobbie followed after her, to her. And we left them in that tree, to wait until we were gone and all was still and safe for them to climb down.

On the way back, up the long, steep canyon in the pickup truck, Pat was quiet. Bobbie had scratched himself a little place in her heart. An occupational hazard. Worry is always the last thing to go when friends part forever.

"He'll be just fine," I smiled. Pat suddenly looked up and smiled back, a glint in her eyes, a reflection in mine.

The best rule of friendship is to keep your heart a little softer than your head.

A REAL LION HUNT is when you bring them back alive.

Just a week ago I was sitting at my desk at the Monterey, California, SPCA when the radio dispatcher buzzed me on the intercom. A mountain lion had been hit by a car. It was 2:45 p.m. and the beginning of 24 hours that I am unlikely to ever forget.

I alerted Pat Quinn, the SPCA's wildlife director, and she loaded equipment into our rescue truck while I got tranquilizer drugs from the veterinarian in our spay clinic. Always be ready for the unexpected when you're dealing with an injured wild animal. We took a large portable cage, ropes, nooses, some blankets and the first-aid kit. Our officer in the field had requested the "9-81 gun," so we also took the long-range tranquilizer rifle and the short-range blowgun.

Then we were on the road. Over the truck radio we learned that the big cat was lying in a dense thicket of willows and wild roses. Waiting for us at the site were six police cars, the local game warden, several reporters from nearby newspapers who monitor police radio bands, and the people who had discovered the injured animal.

We had a circus on our hands and we hadn't even arrived. Murphy's Law of Wildlife Rescue: when you have an especially dicey rescue situation — one where it's easy to make mistakes and where someone might get hurt — expect a large and critical audience. Wonderful. And the cat was in the middle of a patch of wild roses. More wonderful still. There goes my new shirt.

When we arrived, Dan Qualls, the SPCA patrol captain who had radioed for help, guided us through a break in the fence and pointed across an open field to where we could see a cluster of police uniforms. The cat was still lying in the thicket and hadn't moved, he said. He thought we could get close enough to use the blowgun. That was fine with me. It is gentler on an animal than the rifle. Besides, I don't like to "shoot" anything.

Dan loaded the syringes for me while Pat and I went to look things over. Tom Pedersen, the game warden, told us about the large dried blood splotch up on the road and pointed to where the cat was. It was about 60 feet away and I could just barely make out the huge tan form in the shadows. The lion was lying on its side facing us. Even at that distance, when I made eye contact it hissed at me.

Pat and I slowly crawled to within about 15 feet and squatted to talk things over. From the sunken appearance of the animal's hindquarters I suspected a broken back, but then I saw the tail twitch. I felt better. As my eyes got used to the shadows, I began to see the extent of the injuries. Bare bone was sticking out in the middle of the left hind leg. When the cat shifted slightly it exposed the other hind leg and that was broken, too. From the haunted look in the big cat's eyes and the way the lids drooped when I wasn't moving closer, I knew it was very dehydrated and in shock.

"It's going to be a close one," Pat whispered.

Pat and I take turns on rescues like this and this one was mine. I had Dan load a dart with half the normal dose. We had to be very careful.

My first dart glanced off a willow branch and missed. I eased in closer, twisting and scraping through the rose thorns until I was only six feet away. The big cat's eyes followed my every move and the snarls grew louder. It raised its body on those powerful forelegs and tensed.

My second dart hit perfectly in the meaty part of the thigh. The cat responded with a paralyzing scream and slapped out with those great paws. I lunged awkwardly backwards through the grasping roses, stumbling off-balance as Pat caught me under the arms to keep me from nosediving into the grass. My dive away from the lion was pure reflex. I have huge respect for those animals.

I smiled back at Pat, "We've got to stop meeting like this."

But I needn't have worried. The cat wasn't going anywhere. It was still on its side, a snarl on its beautiful face, the tranquilizer dart with its glow-pink cotton tail sprouting like a new spring wildflower from its haunch. Even as it hissed at me again I could see the great head starting to nod.

Pat and I slowly crawled back into the thicket. The lion's head rested peacefully on a log and its eyes were closed. I brushed a twig against the whiskers. There was no response.

The lion was a young male, about 2 years old and between 75 and 100 pounds. He was magnificent. Just to be in such close proximity was a lifetime thrill, until you saw his back legs. They were broken — compound fractures of both tibias where the car had run over them. I could see mud plugging the end of one of the big bones.

Together we eased the beast onto our improvised stretcher — a large blanket — and, each gripping a rolled up side, slid him out of the thicket.

We looked up to find six shotguns pointing at us.

After I had swallowed my heart, I gave the police officers a disgusted look. They sheepishly shrugged and lowered their guns. Not all the dangers in this work come from the animals.

The game warden helped us load the heavy cat into the cage in the back of our truck. Pat carefully folded a blanket under the sleeping head and gently covered the animal's body with another. On the way back to Monterey we radioed ahead to alert our veterinary hospital and the doctors that we were coming in with a critical patient.

All the way back we discussed how to handle the case. Pat's eyes kept checking the lion. He slept all the way to the hospital. You watch the chest and your heart stops with each breath, waiting for another.

"Can you fix him up so we can rehabilitate him back into the wild?" My standard question to Tom Williams, our vet. My heart was in my throat. The legs looked bad, although looks don't always mean anything; some of the worst-looking injuries are the simplest to fix, and conversely what you can't see will sometimes be fatal.

If the vet can't patch up the cat so we can give it back its freedom, we will give him painless eternal sleep. We're not in the business of making captive cripples.

Tom thoughtfully returned my look. He knew what I was thinking. "I think we have a chance. But no promises. I can plate the breaks. Infection's going to be the biggie. If we can lick that, I think he'll make it. But no promises."

By 5 p.m. the cat was starting to wake up from my injection, so we put a plastic mask over his muzzle and sent him back to sleep with a breath of halothane, an anesthetic gas. We X-rayed his legs from all angles and then took pictures of his abdomen and chest for good measure. No telling what other damage that hit-and-run car might have caused.

While the X-rays were developing, we moved the lion into the prep room and Tom and his surgical nurses started cleaning out the wounds — shaving off stiff fur and digging mud out of the bones. "This injury is at least three days old, you know," Tom muttered bitterly. "They hit him and left him lying there. If they'd called someone we could have been doing this three critical days ago." He sighed.

The X-rays showed no other injuries. Heartening. After cleaning the dirt out of the damaged area, they washed the wounds with surgical soap and then injected antibiotics. At the same time, intravenous fluids were steadily being pumped into his dehydrated body. As Tom finished packing and bandaging both legs, Pat asked him when he planned to do the surgery. "Noon to-morrow," he replied. "We'll get him rehydrated tonight and I'll operate tomorrow."

At 8 p.m. we left the lion sleeping quietly in a large holding cage, turned out the lights and locked up the hospital. It had been a long day. We were all exhausted.

That night as I lay awake in my bed, I wondered. Do those big cats ever dream like us? Do they run in their sleep and leap and chase deer? Do their legs twitch as the mind climbs that old oak at the top of the hill to stretch across that big limb and stare off into the distance with half-opened eyes? I finally fell asleep. In my dreams I saw him lying in that oak.

At 8 a.m. the next morning I phoned the hospital. Great news! The lion was alert and hissing at everyone. And peeing like crazy. The fluids we were pouring into him were doing their job. The rest of the morning was a busy flurry of treating other injured wildlife being brought in to our rescue center.

They had given the cat another bedtime shot and he was snoozing again at midday when we arrived at the hospital. Dr. Tom intubated him, adding a mixture of halothane and oxygen, and we lifted him onto the operating table while the surgeon and his nurses scrubbed up. "We'll do the hard leg first," said Tom with a grin. "It'll give us confidence."

It went like clockwork. He made the first incision. The ends of the bone fitted together perfectly. You could make out Tom's delighted grin through the tight surgical mask. For Pat and me it was a time of frustration. The cat now belonged to the surgeon. Our time would come again during the long recovery.

Tom drilled holes, laid the stainless steel plate along the top of the leg bone to bridge the broken gap, and screwed in the screws. They fitted snug and tight. The bones were aligned perfectly. He finished with the first leg and started suturing it up. Time for the other leg. We were halfway there. And this one would go much faster.

"Doctor?"

The silence was deafening. Pat and I were sitting on the floor just outside the operating room. We jumped to our feet. All eyes jerked to the monitor. The cat's heart had stopped.

Tom immediately started giving external heart massage. One nurse turned off the anesthesia gas and squeezed the rubber bag to force pure oxygen into the cat's lungs. Tom told another nurse to bring heart stimulant, ripped off his surgical mask, grabbed the syringe and felt for the heart. He plunged in the needle, drew back on the plunger until he saw the rich dark heart blood, injected the stimulant, then dropped the needle to the floor and went back to massaging the lion's chest.

He was perspiring. He stopped to listen to the cat's chest with his stethoscope, then called for another shot. "Come on, you . . . " he pleaded anxiously. "Don't stop now!"

Between a good surgeon and his nurse there is almost extrasensory understanding. The look was so quick I nearly missed it. He just glanced up at her, then back down at the cat. She turned and flipped off the oxygen, then started methodically switching off the other instruments. Tom stood there looking down, drained, eyes red and brimmed with moisture. Everyone was suddenly looking everywhere but at each other.

I looked up at the clock. It was 2:45 p.m., exactly 24 hours since we had gotten that first call that a mountain lion had been injured by a stupid car. Twenty-four hours. It seemed like a lifetime. It was.

As I looked down at the soft body as it sprawled stiffly across the steel table, I remembered my dream of the night before. I saw the great vibrant form draped across that big oak limb, the twin glints winking mockingly at me through the half-closed lids.

Do mountain lions dream? I hope so. Because that tree was his forever.

A WALK ON THE WILD SIDE with a frisky cougar cub.

You're doubtless familiar with walking the dog, but consider what it's like to take a mountain lion out on an early morning stroll.

A young cub needs plenty of exercise, especially if you want to raise him strong enough to return to the wild. And the early hours are a good, quiet, unobtrusive time. (If you're walking a lion near town, it's best to be unobtrusive.)

Sioux, our cub, enjoys the really windy days above all others. The winds seem to gust away whatever barriers of civilization we've inadvertently raised in his young mind. For him a little sip of wind is quite intoxicating.

I drive the van through the early, empty streets; the first glint of the awakening sun winks at us over Mount Diablo.

As we near our special field, Sioux poses himself on the seat, stiff and taut like an ancient harpooner in the pulpit of a plunging whaler, head held high to face the breeze, eyes tightly squinting against the spray, sturdy feet spread wide against the pitch and roll.

He is too proud to lower his haughty gaze and acknowledge the startled commuter whose car is nearly merging with our van, but the slight lowering of one ear signals his delight at this ability to confuse and confound with a single curling of a claw against the window.

Because of the cat riding in my passenger seat, more than one hot cup of early morning coffee has ended up in a surprised driver's lap.

Our field: a sea of swelling, smelling mustard plants, green-stemmed beauties that reach as high as my chin and swirl in the wind like the emerald waters of a windward tidepool. The yellow flowers are like thick foam as the pollen loosens with our passing and fills the air with spindrift.

A light wind joins us; the grasses surge into a swell of mighty waves that build and roll around us, making me crouch or look down until the dizziness goes away.

Sioux is instantly away as we enter the mustard waters. He dives into those murky depths and disappears with a swirl of yellow fog.

I range out, stroking through the surf, and the game is on. It's very simple, really: The cat hides in the deep grass, stalking me by sound, by scent, as I try in turn to confuse him, and to anticipate his sudden, frightening rushes.

The heavy, clinging stems pull against the cat's chest to make this a difficult, violent exercise for him. It's like running through thick, starchy spaghetti, pulling, straining, toning young muscles. It's difficult to ascertain just who's more exhausted at the end of these runs, the cat or the man.

In this game you have to be able to read the signs. Red-winged blackbirds nest in the middle of this green jungle, and they become disturbed at the predator's passing.

Nature is reckless of the individual. When she has points to carry, she carries them.
— Emerson ("Culture")

15

Presently an area is completely ringed by these red-and-black beaters, and you know something lurks in this seemingly vacant patch of fodder.

You notice a gently nodding flower; maybe it's him. Maybe it's the wind. Maybe he's really behind you, waiting to leap . . . or to the side . . .

One has sudden sympathy for the deer.

Then the charge.

His body creates a foaming yellow wake; a living torpedo is seeking your flimsy side, and without thinking you automatically turn and start to run, your legs suddenly have developed a will of their own; for that one frantic, primitive instant you are the mindless prey.

As you panic and dash left, then right, checking back with quick looks, you catch sight of the foaming wake as it relentlessly veers with your every move. Almost anticipating your every move. And the age-old fear leaks through, and with each closing foot you uncontrollably become more frantic, and your panting lunges against the grasping grasses dissolve into a stumble as he finally comes bursting from the green shadows to wrap around your knees and take you down.

Filled with sanity once again, we lie together, side by side, gasping painfully for breath, all sides heaving up and down, panting, my laughter mingling with his heavy rumbling purrs, steam rising in misty clouds from our dewy, overheated bodies.

Then a sudden ripple in the greenness leaves me alone again, and that intelligent wake fades again into the depths.

The morning is also good for walking a man.

EVERY SONGDOG HAS HIS DAY before fading into the night.

The coyote pup pressed and pressed with all his little might, straining to make his terrified body somehow pass through the chain-link fence. But cold steel can hold even the warm, carefree spirit of the songdog.

He was hard caught, a prisoner in a human's cage.

The little varmint was about 5 months old, and roughly the size of a German shepherd of the same age. But if you had yourself a dog that skinny, whose eyes continually flickered here, there, and every which way but loose, with ears that never stopped looking (even backward), and a body that flinched visibly as if the slightest sound were a physical blow — you'd swear it was sick, near to death, maybe ready for the crazy house.

Just your average penned-up coyote.

But this frightened pup was a survivor. All sinew, long tendons and runner's muscle, slant eyes that saw things before they happened, ears that tracked the wind, and electric reflexes that sparked with a mind of their own.

He'd been shot — an occupational hazard for the working coyote — but the bullet had only creased his head, dazing him. It blazed a track between the ears that seemed to part his hair right down the middle.

A man who witnessed the shooting picked him up and brought him to me for help.

At first the coyote lived in a dream world. You could walk up to the side of his cage and he would just cock his head like the RCA Victor dog and look off in some other direction for his master's voice. He saw everything in reverse. I'd be over here and he'd look for me over there. That bullet really scrambled his brains.

Sometimes he stared straight at you, straight through you as if you didn't exist in the same world. Other times he slept so soundly you could march into his cage, change his water, bang the dish, and march right back out without waking him. His ears slept, too; when that happens to a coyote, he's really out.

But after those first lost days he improved. He'd hear you coming around the side of the house and before you even got close enough to see him you'd hear a crash and a thump and you'd know he was hiding in the wooden doghouse in back of the cage.

But today he didn't hide. He knew. They always know when something is up. And as these creatures often do, he'd stayed to face openly whatever came.

I approached him slowly, one measured step at a time, bending down as I crept. *Easy old pardner, easy old son.* His eyes pinned mine, and as I squatted down, still whispering, his teeth flashed just once for show. My left hand gently touched his hard flank and his eyes slowly rolled up and closed, his body stiffened so hard it quiv-

Nature is often hidden, sometimes overcome, seldom extinguished.
— Francis Bacon ("Of Nature In Men")

ered. His sides heaved to a gasping breath as he waited for the end.

. I eased him into the darkness of a traveling box.

I took him to the top of a grassy hill overlooking a canyon with deep, brushy sides and a thick, oak-tree bottom. A whisper of wind swept bird voices around us.

The little coyote blinked rapidly as the early morning sun screamed into his matching yellow eyes. He shook his head once in disbelief, started to look about, then froze again as he saw my legs at his side.

Then, suddenly aware of his freedom, shocked down to his tailhairs that he was still alive, the little coyote lunged frantically down the hill, crashing through crackling brittle brush, hissing past protesting dry grasses; his tail high, rippling like a banner in the wind. His mouth wide in a coyote smile, teeth flashing a grin as he sucked mouthfuls of sweet, free air. He barked like a dog and surprised us both with the strength of his elation. Then he was gone, leaving the harsh *rasp, rasp* of a startled jay in his wake.

I sat awhile, savored that moment of mutual joy, and basked with a lizard in the warm morning sun.

A WILEY COYOTE has a lot of tricks up his sleeves.

Wiley was a good old coyote.

Eight years ago, Wiley had the misfortune to be born with his name on the surplus list at a local zoo. Translated, that meant something had to go — Wiley and his squirming litter mates. Too many coyotes in one spot, even if it's just a zoo, tends to make people nervous.

The thinning procedure is usually accomplished these days with a painless injection. In the not-so-distant past a knock on the head was traditional. But Wiley the coyote was destined for greater things.

On the day of his scheduled execution, I happened to be visiting the zoo with Bobbie Meyer, a staff member at our museum. When we got into the van to leave, Bobbie had a fuzzy gray bundle snoozing on her lap — Wiley, the survivor.

So Wiley moved in with Bobbie and her family. At first he had the run of the house, but when he started to grow they built him a large run to live and play in. Every day they took him on long walks in the nearby hills. They all quickly grew to love each other; it wasn't long before old Wiley coyote was an official member of the Meyer family. And Wiley even got a job.

Each spring the wildlife rescue team at our museum gets a batch or three of orphaned coyote pups. A few years back the ranchers used to dump in gasoline to burn out the dens around here. They still do when nobody's looking. But nowadays some just dig up the cubs and give them to the game warden to bring to us — if we cross our hearts and swear not to release them back on the ranch they came from. You can bank on us.

So we take the cubs from rancher Jones and release them in the dead of night on the Smith Ranch. And we take all the cubs brought to us by rancher Smith and release them in the dead of night on the Jones Ranch. So we still have a healthy supply of coyotes at our end of the county. But if you were to ask, I'd deny it.

Eight years ago, when Bobbie first got Wiley, the science of raising and training those little displaced canines for release back into the wild hadn't even been invented.

It's not so difficult to show little coyotes how to hunt. That sort of stuff comes pretty naturally. Socializing is the hard thing to learn in captivity. Wild coyotes are a gregarious bunch and the youngsters need to be taught how to get along with their elders. Otherwise one of them's going to get his little butt bit off someday when he doesn't mind his manners.

And there's howling. Let us certainly not forget the howling. Somebody's got to teach the little critters how to howl.

Well, I suspect you've already guessed it. Curious fellow that I am, I wondered what would happen if we stuck one of those little orphans in with Wiley. And maybe being a little bit dumb at times but not eter-

There is no wealth but life.
— John Ruskin,
Unto This Last (1862)

nally stupid, I picked a cute little female coyote for the experiment. And it worked.

Wiley raised her as his own daughter and kept her nice and wild. They raised voice together in nightly ballads to the moon.

And so we raised that little motherless lass, or Wiley did. And she grew up wild and strong and wise in the ways of coyotes. And then we took her out and released her. Because of a funny mark on her coat we were able to recognize her from time to time and to know that she was coping well with her freedom.

That was eight years ago. Since that time, Wiley's children have grown to number more than 20. And his grandchildren? There surely must be a passel. Maybe two passel.

And then, a couple of months ago, Bobbie and her husband John finally did something they'd been thinking about for a long time. They took old Wiley out and released him. He was set free with a young female coyote that he'd raised from last year's batch of wayward pups.

Ah, and they made such a beautiful pair. Old Wiley with his lush, rusty-backed coat, and the little gal so pert, plump and bushy-tailed.

Just before they set off toward the trees where the grass was growing tall and the fat ground squirrels whistled, Wiley turned for one last look at Bobbie and John. His mom and dad.

They all stood there. The tame and the wild. Man and animal. Old friends sharing that happy-sad moment of parting. The sudden face-flushing rush of memories of all the good years past. The friendship and love. All those kids he'd raised.

A final uncertain smile. What might have been a brief wag of a tail. Goodbye and good luck.

SORRY, WRONG NUMBER,
I mumbled into the phone

I got a phone call from Egypt last night.

I groped for the telephone with one hand and turned around the clock with the other. I could barely make out the glowing numerals. Jeeze.

I flopped back onto the pillow, the earpiece jammed against my left ear.

"I have a collect call for Mr. Gary Bogue from Egypt," whispered a high-pitched Southern accent.

I didn't know they talked like that in Egypt.

"Gimme a break, lady," I groaned. "It's 2 a.m.!"

"No, Arkansas," she drawled. "Egypt, Arkansas."

What would they think of next.

"Do you have pyramids?"

"Sir, I have a collect call for Gary Bogue from . . . "

" . . . Egypt, Arkansas," I croaked. "From who?"

"She says you don't know her, sir, but she needs your help and it's a matter of life and death. Will you accept the call?"

You're a newspaper columnist and a mysterious lady you don't know calls you in the middle of the night . . . collect . . . from Egypt, Arkansas. How would you handle it?

"I'll accept the call."

Her voice was shaking and she spoke so fast and low I had to sit up to hear her.

"Is this the Gary Bogue who writes a newspaper column about helping injured wild animals?"

"Sometimes," I replied. "But not in Egypt, Arkansas."

"My mom sends me your columns. They're very good."

"And you're calling me at 2 a.m. to tell me that? Gee . . . "

"I hit a deer," she sobbed. "And I think it's dying . . . and the troopers are here . . . and they want to shoot it . . . and I won't let them . . . and . . . "

"Slow down, lady," I whispered. "Relax. Tell me where you're calling from. How did it happen?"

"A pay phone. I can see it lying there on its back. Its front legs are kicking and it's bleeding."

"Did it run in front of you?"

"It ran into my fender, please . . . " she moaned. "They want to kill it. I don't want to kill that beautiful animal. Please . . . she's alive!"

"Describe it to me. You say its front legs are moving? How about the back legs?" I tried to make my voice crisp, professional. Non-committal."

"The back legs are just lying there. They won't move."

"Does it try to stand up?" I questioned. I could close my eyes and see it lying there. Like I'd seen a hundred other deer lying on a hundred different roads over the years.

"It tries," she sniffed. "But just with its front legs . . . and now it's just lying on its back."

"Can I talk to one of the troopers?" I

We live in deeds, not years; in thoughts, not breaths;
In feelings, not figures on a dial.
— Philip James Bailey

21

asked. "They're experienced with injuries and I need some technical information . . . before we decide what to do."

"Oh thank you! I just knew you'd help it! Wait . . . "

The next voice was definitely an Arkansas state trooper.

"Both hips is mashed up and her back is busted too and she's hurtin' bad and I think we better do it now," said the lanky voice.

"I figured," I said. "You'll have to shoot it . . . but let me talk to the lady some more, first, so I can . . . hello? HELLO?"

He'd hung up.

I sat there staring at the phone, but that's not what I was seeing. I was seeing the broad back of the trooper as he retreat-ed from the phone booth . . . his right hand yank the revolver from its holster to offer the dying doe that final act of mercy . . .

And I could see the lady slumped against the phone booth, crying for the deer she had killed. For the deer she'd thought I was going to save.

Where the hell is Egypt, Arkansas?

I never even learned her name.

Now there's no way I'll ever be able to help her ease her guilt.

Or erase her hate for the man she'd only met in the pages of her mother's newspapers.

But maybe if her mom is still sending her my columns — maybe she'll send her this one.

The one that says I'm sorry.

HELPING HANDS for a fawn in need.

About four in the afternoon, a call came in from the principal of a local elementary school. A tiny fawn had been trapped behind the playground fences surrounding the school; it had been there at least a day and a half.

Fawns are fragile creatures and this one had gone probably 36 hours without food. If we didn't do something now, before dark, the little animal could be dead or dying of exposure and dehydration by morning. Perhaps it was already too late.

Deer are caught behind fences fairly commonly in suburbia. The lush playing fields behind the school buildings stretch across several acres: deep, grassy, brush-covered, tree-lined acres that butt against some steep wild hills. Two nights before, a mama doe and her newborn twins had quietly slipped through an open gate and onto the playing fields that are so much like a big meadow.

The next morning the children and teachers found the deer frantically racing back and forth along that fence, trying to win their way back into the safety of the hills.

The kids finally managed to herd the doe and one fawn back through the gate. But the other fawn lost itself in the brush. It probably dropped like a stone into the deep cool grass — remaining absolutely, invisibly, still — hiding from those frightening creatures until its mother could come back and retrieve it.

But the doe was not on the wrong side of the fence. She couldn't come back to get him to let him nurse, to let him press against her living warmth at night. That little fawn was in very big trouble.

I gave that a lot of thought as I drove to the school with Marcia Fortney, another museum staff member. I looked up at the gray threatening clouds, counted the rain sprinkles on my windshield, and worried. The fawn had been two days and a night without food. It had been severely stressed, chased by well-meaning kids and teachers. Its energy reserves had to be getting awfully low.

And now it would get wet and cold in the rain. Almost 5 p.m. and already getting dark. Not good.

As Marcia and I climbed out of the car I took my long-handled net and she grabbed two big bath towels. My dismay got stronger after a good look at the field — even larger than I'd remembered.

Suddenly we saw, on the far side of the field, a tiny figure waving energetically. Things got blurry and hectic at that point. Impressions, thoughts: Jogging across that endless field; tall grass, blades slashing back at your legs; white faces, concerned, excited teachers; loud breathing sounds; crouching by a tree and looking; standing in deep ivy and pointing.

"Hey . . . down in that grass there. The last place I saw it. It's probably hiding . . . "

Such stillness —
The cries of
the cicadas
Sink into the rocks.
— Matsuo Basho
(1644-1694)

23

Creeping as quietly as you can with your breath coming in ragged gasps and the sweat burning your eyes, a match for the hotness in your chest, still winded from the long dash across the field. *There!* A tiny brown shape explodes at your feet, dribbling in front of you like a basketball that's been knocked from your hands to bounce across the court.

Your legs pound to catch up. Ridiculous dreaming man. That little idiot can run circles around you. Waving arms, grabbing, missing.

"Coming your way, Marcia . . . "

"He's cutting back!"

"Hey, it's gone!"

"Last place I saw it was at that little brown patch of dry grass."

Ah, that patch of dried grass. It had to be there. Fawns can drop to the ground from a dead run and instantly vanish. So what do you do in a case like this? Well, you take your net and you *capture* that dried-out patch of grass.

And it *explodes* into lunging, frantic, screaming fawn!

I grasp it firmly, gently, press it tight against my chest, whisper into a curly, velvet ear. Marcia's soft hands carefully explore the body for hurts. Her eyes quickly check some superficial cuts on its face (from its run-in with the fence). Nothing serious.

"Look!" someone shouts. "Up the hill!"

It's the doe, drawn from hiding by the screams of her frightened fawn. She stands tall and brown against the green, ears pointing like accusing fingers, nostrils flared, confused. Afraid.

I find myself running again, toward the fence. If the doe charges the fence she could injure herself. Quickly I drop the fawn over; it bounces up the hill. The doe cuts across the slopes; two green wakes on an intersecting course.

On the way back to the car, we turn for a last look, just in time to see the doe pass through a clearing. Just barely visible above the tall grass, behind her — a tiny head with two very happy ears.

It feels good.

DON'T BUG ME! You big louse!

Everyone crazy enough to be in the wildlife rescue profession develops sooner or later a personal pet peeve about one thing that keeps the job from being absolutely perfect. In my case this has to do with little annoyances that sometimes get more than slightly out of hand. I will put it more accurately: they get all *OVER* your hand, *AND* body, *AND* into your beard, if you happen to have one.

I refer to fleas, ticks, mites, lice, biting flies. No matter what species of animal you're treating, no matter what its problem might be, such tiny parasitic devils have a nasty way of cree-e-e-ping into the picture when you least expect them.

For instance, a nice lady brought me an old shoebox containing a baby orphaned blackbird. "Oh the poor thing," she exclaims as I gently lift the bird from the box and cup it in my palms to warm its cold little body.

"Thanks for taking the time to rescue it from your cat," I grimace as an all-too-familiar tingling starts flowing across the backs of my hands, oozing onto my wrists, pulsating up my arms.

The tingling is caused, of course, by the rampaging horde of almost microscopic black mites that have deserted the bird's feathers like rats leaving a sinking ship and are trooping up my arms like an elite climbing team attacking the north face of Everest . . . in search of . . . Gary Bogue's beard!

Fortunately, bird parasites are species-specific, meaning they nibble only on birds. But I know from personal experience that they will *CRAWL* on anything!

Don't get me wrong. Not all animals are as parasite-ridden as this. Only the ones I always seem to get to handle.

Last week at my job with the Monterey, California, SPCA's Wildlife Rescue Center, I finally came close to chucking it all. For a while it was touch and go — mostly touch. The little devils almost got the best of me.

It was a busy day. Several deer had been hit by cars and needed care. And a number of the orphaned young deer we'd been raising needed to be tranquilized and transported to a beautiful little valley where they could continue to roam and nibble green leaves and grow into wild adult deer.

It was my turn to ride in the back of the truck with the snoring animals. Halfway to where we were going, one of them started to feel the bumping road in its dreams and woke up. In this kind of situation you do what has to be done. I threw my body over the animal and hung on for dear life, legs wrapped around the animal's powerful hind quarters, to keep my teeth from getting kicked into tomorrow by those deadly hooves; straining arms around the strong young body and the surging forelegs to control them. And I buried my face into its neck to press the deer's thrashing head against my upper arms so it wouldn't bang against the floor of the truck.

All Nature wears one universal grin.
— Henry Fielding
(1707-1754)

This happened all at once. One minute I'm idly overseeing my sleeping charges, the next hanging on with everything I've got. It's not easy in the back of a bouncing truck.

Deer are hard to tranquilize. Each time, they react differently to the drug. That's why Pat and I flip coins and take turns riding in the back. The loser always rides in back with the deer. The task is often bruising. But Pat keeps reassuring me that one of these days she'll let ME flip the coin.

We got there and unloaded the animals and I see Pat looking at me and starting to laugh. I looked down and shuddered. Deer sometimes have a certain species of louse swarming on them in huge numbers. The tiny pests hang onto their victim with their forelegs, and their fat, red abdomens stick straight up into the air. (Three guesses as to why their abdomens are red. Hint: it has to do with something they eat.) I call them "redtails" or "stick-tights."

I've been known to call them other things. Lots of other things. As I did this time, because I was covered with thousands of them, from head to foot, shirt to pants. Cloth gives them a marvelous surface to cling to. And they LOVE corduroy pants. They can hide down in the little grooves. And under your socks. Boy, do they like to get under your socks! And, of course, into my ever-popular beard.

It took me half an hour to pick them off — most of them. My patrolling fingers were still finding little pockets of resistance the next day.

That afternoon, just at 5 when it was supposed to be time to go home, Mark, the radio dispatcher, received a call that there was a brown pelican down on Monterey Wharf with its head caught in a plastic six-pack holder. This always happens to me at closing time.

A popular restaurant is at the end of the Wharf. You can climb the stairs on one side of the building to the roof, where you can gaze out over Monterey Bay and harbor and watch the rainbow fishing boats setting gold crab pots and the sea otters and sea lions cavorting in the clear water.

That particular evening, looking down over the south side of the roof, or up from your table in the dining room and out through the large picture windows, you could also see this idiot being chased around the tables in the patio of the restaurant next door by an angry brown pelican.

Finally I caught the pelican and straddled him with my knees to hold him gently with my legs while I cut the plastic off his bill. I felt over his wings and legs. Since nothing seemed to be broken, I stood and released him so he could take off into the sunset like a good little brown pelican and get out of my life. Only, this fellow had been entangled for so long in that miserable piece of plastic that he didn't have the energy to hop up on the patio wall and sail off across the bay.

But he did have enough energy to run around and start chasing me, as if I were personally responsible for his problem.

Having been introduced on previous occasions to the sharp tip of a pelican's beak, I wasn't about to let him catch me. So we did a few laps around the tables until I was able to maneuver him into a position where I could grab the sword-like bill and take charge. I figured the pelican could use a few days at the SPCA to fatten up and regain his strength.

As I grabbed the long bill in one hand, tucked his large body under my right arm, and turned to head back to my truck, I was suddenly aware of loud cheering, shouting, whistling, stomping, and applause. Looking up in surprise and shock, I discovered my audience hanging over the side of the restaurant roof and lining the windows of the dining room, Nikons and Brownies clicking away.

Suddenly my face felt very hot, and I looked frantically around for a convenient hole to crawl into. Only you don't crawl into a hole on a wharf unless you want to take a swim in the bay. So I bent down and gave a low, sweeping bow to the appreciative crowd. In doing so, I unconsciously released the pelican's beak, allowing him to reach back and take a large hunk out of my right buttock.

Wincing while pretending not to notice (not wanting to ruin my suddenly acquired macho image by screaming), I began to feel an all-too-familiar tingling on both arms. No, actually it was more of a scratchy, methodical, crawling sensation. Those brown pelicans are enormous. And so are their lousy lice!

I think I'm going to ask for an extra $50 in our budget next year for "sanitation supplies."

A case of flea collars.

SOME DAYS YOU JUST CAN'T WIN but still you have to try.

It strikes me that in my discourses on the rescue, care and rehabilitation of distressed wild animals that I may have been somewhat misleading to you. Looking back over these last few years, it seems that I usually write about the positive aspects of my work, about successful rescues, about animals we have saved and returned to the wild. Sometimes it is well to report the negative side. It keeps things in perspective.

Actually, if you must know the truth, I had a lousy couple of days recently and feel like talking about it. The wildlife rescue business can do this to you. Lots of trauma cases, gunshot wounds, starving animals. You lose many, and it gets to you.

One of the most frustrating things about this work is the lack of proper rescue equipment — of means of helping animals without causing further injury to man or beast. Some things we need simply haven't been invented. It's still a young field. Besides, you never have the funds you need to buy something even if it is available. All wildlife rescue centers are non-profit — and I mean *really* non-profit.

People who survive in this work do so by becoming professional con-artists. Oops! Did I say that? I don't want to offend anybody so I'd better reword that. Let's just say they're good at persuading people to lend a hand. Anyway, that's what started my problems last week.

It had been an extra-long day. Animals had died during the night, so the morning body count was up. One of the brown pelicans we released in the afternoon had suddenly developed a new problem (Murphy's Law of Animal Rescue). It couldn't extend its right wing all the way (even though it had done so regularly in our large flight aviary!) and thus couldn't fly. But it could still paddle out into the middle of Monterey Bay, where it bobbed and thumbed its big beak at us. Pat looked over at me in disgust. We both knew that feathered freeloader would probably beat us back to our clinic for the evening feeding.

At 4 p.m. the calls started coming in. I'd been half-expecting it. Something always happens just before closing time. A gull was entangled in fishing line and floating about 100 feet offshore at Otter Point in Monterey. Just close enough to shore for the tourists to line the rocky beach and wring their hands in dismay. Every time the gull tried to swim, it would bob under water. The sheriff's dispatcher called, pleading. Their switchboard was buckling under the load of calls about the gull. And police cars can't drive on water.

We had our own problem — no boat. We'd been pulling our hair out for weeks trying to figure a way to get a rubber Zodiac with a motor, old or new and small and maneuverable, for close-in rescues like this.

So old tarnished-silver-tongue here stared at the wall for a minute, then phoned the local U.S. Coast Guard Search and Rescue Unit and somehow got them to agree to order out a patrol and crew, on the condition that we accompany them to handle the killer gull. I figured it was sheer coincidence that it was also time for their boat to go out on patrol.

I was feeling pretty smug as Pat and I drove to the Coast Guard base. I had visions of a 40-foot white charger racing to the rescue of a damsel sea gull in distress, and of busloads of tourists clicking away with their cameras as the heroic wildlife rescue team feverishly gnawed the tangle of fishing line off the bird with our bare teeth.

We arrived at the Coast Guard pier and rushed to meet the crew of our rescue craft, appreciative smiles on our faces. Three women stared coldly back at us. One carried a shotgun, another had a .45 automatic strapped to her waist. I'd forgotten that these guardians of the coast always go out armed in case of dope smugglers.

"You the people who want us to waste taxpayers' money going out after some blankety-blank sea gull?" snarled the one with the .45 automatic.

Pat and I tugged on our life preservers and stood as far apart from the crew as we could without falling overboard. They gunned the boat a couple of times and we sped out around the breakwater and into the bay at full throttle, with Pat and I wrapped around the railing and hanging on for dear life.

When we reached the last reported location of the gull, the boat pulled in tight to shore. We all lined up along the side, scanning the glassy, kelp-clogged waters. The gal with the .45 on her belt was beside me.

My eyes searched the water frantically. I had this funny feeling that if we didn't come up with that gull they were *really* going to be angry.

I felt a sharp tapping on my back. "They just radioed that your gull was rescued by somebody else," she gritted, turning back to stand in front of the cabin door with the rest of the crew.

Taking a deep breath and setting my shoulders, I strode across the burning deck to see what I could do to salvage something from this fiasco. Gathering every trick I had left in my seabag of golden oratory, I opened my mouth to thank the nice ladies for helping us. "Uh, gee, thanks ... *guys.*"

Believe it or not, by the time we got back to shore we were all the best of friends. My verbal gaffe had luckily broken the ice. By the time they all stopped laughing at my red face, and Pat and I had explained what we were all about (meaning that we also helped things besides blankety-blank gulls), everyone was happy. Our crew promised to keep an eye out for injured wildlife on future patrols.

It was 6:30 p.m. when we got back. So ended a day beset by frustration, maybe a little fear (OK, so I thought they were going to shoot us and dump us overboard) and plain old nervous exhaustion.

It didn't improve things when the SPCA's night animal control officer phoned me at 1 a.m. to ask for a hand with a deer that had been hit by a truck. Especially when the animal died before we got there.

At 2:30 a.m. I was back in bed wondering what I was doing in this business besides growing old very fast. At 5 a.m. I finally got tired of tossing and turning and got up to make coffee and try to figure out why I'm always so tired in the morning.

Just before lunchtime the Fish and Game department's marine warden called to say one of his biologists had spotted two sea lions out on the end of the rocky jetty by the Coast Guard pier. He said both were cut and bleeding, with fish net wound tightly around their heads. They were in bad trouble, meaning they would die unless they got help.

Oh God, please don't make me call the Coast Guard again!

Fortunately it developed that the fish and game biologist had a boat and was on hand to help.

I phoned our vet, a specialist in marine mammal care, and asked him what drug we should use. He named one. I asked how the sea lions would react to it. He didn't know. Big help you are, I say. Not much is known about tranquilizing sea lions in the wild, he replies. Yeah, I say, but we could end up killing one of those animals. That's right, he responds, but they are going to die a particularly horrible death if you don't try something. If they drown, at least they'll go quickly. Nobody asked you to get into this work, he adds. Our vet always likes to get in the last word.

Pat and I loaded our nets, blankets and dart guns into the boat and sat in the bow. Dan, the SPCA patrol captain, sat behind us fiddling with his air-rifle. The biologist spun the wheel and sent us put-putting along the jetty, heading for the congregation of sea lions — a jumble of brown bodies on the rocks out on the point.

As we chugged past the Coast Guard dock, I looked up and saw our crew of the day before, cleaning their boat. We exchanged friendly waves. "Going out after another blankety-blank sea gull?" called one of the gals with a grin. Don't I wish, I thought.

Until recently, injured sea lions were caught by waiting for them to crawl up on the beach. We had to dream up a way to get them more quickly, while they were still strong enough for us to treat them and pull them through. Pat and I had talked it over. All we had to do was take this drug, shoot the lions with the tranquilizer rifle from the deck of a tiny, tossing boat, then somehow keep the animals from plunging into the ocean and sinking unconscious to the bottom, where they would drown. Then we had to load those 200-pound-plus deadweights back into the boat without capsizing it and drowning us all, clip the nets away and treat the injuries on the spot, or at the vet's if they were serious.

And finally get the sea lions back to their rocks and freedom.

How come Marlin Perkins never has such problems?

Dan's shot hit the first sea lion smack in the large muscles of the shoulder. This is the kind of shot you want. If you hit where the animal is thinly muscled, the thick needle on the end of the dart can break bones. The animal and all 15 or so others lounging around her immediately dove off the rocks and began swimming around our boat. She wasn't hard to spot, with her monofilament halo, so we grabbed the dip net and started watching for the effects of the drug. We were still watching when we suddenly noticed she hadn't come up from her last dive.

Fifteen minutes later we realized the worst. She was gone. Nowhere to be seen on the rocks, nowhere in the water. Maybe she had swum to another beach. Yes, that was it. She went somewhere else. Pat and I looked at each other. We both glanced back down into the murky green depths. Maybe she'd turn up. Maybe she wouldn't. We'd have to live with that.

The other injured animal was in even worse shape than the first. Her head was a thick ball of fuzzy nylon netting, and she was bony from lack of food. We could easily see where the sharp cords had cut deep into her neck, causing blood to flow down the sides. But she was alone and far back on the rocks along the middle of the jetty. This time we had a better chance.

Again Dan's shot was on target. The animal stopped on a shallow ledge and sat watching us. We drifted back to wait. Five minutes, 10, 20. You never see this on "Wild Kingdom" because it gets cut out of the film. At 25 minutes we were figuring the drug wasn't going to work when, suddenly, the sea lion plunged for the depths. A second later she screamed up into the air, breaching gracefully like a whale and falling back into the water on her side with a great splash. She repeated this again and again. One second she would dive. Thirty seconds later she would be 100 yards away and breaching, then suddenly 100 yards off

in another direction. The drug, rather than putting her to sleep, had totally agitated her, freaked her out. Wonderful! Even tried and true tranquilizer drugs used in animal rescue sometimes cause totally unexpected results. It doesn't make it easy.

Once we almost caught her when she was cartwheeling across the surface. Pat's lunge missed by inches and nearly sent her headfirst into the water with the animal.

Five minutes later the frenzy quieted as quickly as it had started. The sea lion was back up on the rocks, looking a bit dazed and perhaps wondering what the commotion was all about. And noticeably weaker. It had taken a lot out of her.

So it went. Tomorrow we'd have to try again with something else. And tomorrow we'd probably have to go scrounging for a new boat, since it would be the biologist's day off. Maybe that first sea lion would also be back on her rock so we could have another try at helping her. I hoped so.

The next morning both animals, their heads still enmeshed in strands of netting, were indeed back at the end of the jetty. That was at least one fear removed — we hadn't killed them in our attempts to help.

Unfortunately, we were never able to get close to them again. After several weeks both disappeared and they were never reported thereafter. They left us all with a feeling of guilt because we hadn't been able to help.

Maybe next time.

That's what keeps you going.

It is the marriage of the soul with Nature that makes intellect fruitful, and gives birth to imagination. — Thoreau, Journal, Aug. 21, 1851

A CLOSE ENCOUNTER OF THE BEST KIND

A young gray whale recently became entangled in fish netting in San Francisco Bay. This was only the latest in a series of curious, even mysterious encounters between man and sea mammals along the California coastline this year. Mysterious because in one bay in a single month, three dolphins, along with the young gray whale, have needed man's help to survive.

The young whale was cut free and herded back to sea by a boatload of seagoing "animal control officers" — the U.S. Coast Guard. I became involved with the dolphins while consulting in Monterey with the local SPCA's wildlife rescue team.

I'll be honest about it. I had worked with many species of wild animals over the years, but never a dolphin. I had seen them in the shows at Marine World, and I used to watch Flipper on TV faithfully when I was a youngster. But I'd never before been close enough to touch one. Or to stare one in the eye. Or to hear its plaintive cry of distress. Or to feel it tremble and sigh beneath my hand.

We had just dropped an injured fawn off at the vet's when a call came over the truck radio that a dolphin was stranded on Del Monte Beach near historic Monterey Wharf. In the distance, as we drove down the packed beach sand, the animal looked like a huge sculptured piece of blue driftwood. The young lady who'd found the dolphin was desperately pouring water on it from a tiny plastic glass, the only thing she'd had in her purse. The dolphin was already above the waterline — the tide was going out. The woman and a man had tried to shove it back into the water but it kept turning and driving itself back up on the beach.

She was sobbing softly and kept running down to the water and filling her tiny glass and running back and pouring that little splash onto the drying back of the giant mammal.

Why do dolphins do that? What makes a living, vibrant, intelligent creature propel itself out of its element to lie gasping under the hot sun with its skin rapidly drying under the dehydrating ocean breezes? Some scientists say the cause is parasites in the inner ear confusing the dolphin's sense of direction. Others blame some sort of stress, perhaps illness. No one knows for sure. And it might not be the same reason each time. But sometimes hundreds of sleek dolphins and whole families of gentle whales will run up on a lonely beach and lie stranded until they die.

To make our particular incident even more curious, we hadn't had a dolphin on the beach in over a year. Now suddenly we had one, and the next week another, and the next still another. None had any visible wound. All looked of normal weight. And how beautiful they were.

To make it more mysterious, this was a common dolphin, *Delphinus delphis*, not normally seen this far north of the warm waters of Baja California. What was it doing here in the cold? Local fishermen later reported a school of 50 of this species just offshore.

We got the sheets from the truck, wet them in the waves, and draped them over the dolphin. The ocean-dwellers quickly sunburn if not shaded, and they must be kept wet. We got the buckets — traded one to a now-smiling young lady for her glass — and kept a steady waterfall of cool ocean pouring over its body.

It was weak. Each breath — a sudden explosive gasp of warm, curiously sweet-smelling fog from the blowhole in its forehead — came only twice a minute. Its tail would occasionally pat the wet sand with sharp little smacking sounds as if it were dreaming of speeding once again through crystal waters. Both eyelids were sealed shut with a thick coating of mucus.

I bent down very close with that little plastic glass of cool water and poured it gently over one eye and carefully used my finger to loosen the slimy crust. As I did so, the eye suddenly opened and I found myself exchanging stares with another intelligent animal. Our eyes only met for a few seconds. But when two souls first touch, the shock of it can make it into an eternity. Then the dolphin made its first sound since our arrival. A quavering high-pitched cry, like the mewing of a scrawny little kitten. A plea for help.

About half an hour after we'd shaded the dolphin from the sun and started wetting it, its condition began improving. The breathing became more frequent and regu-

lar. Its eyes, cleared of the mixture of sand and mucus, stayed open, and we frequently found ourselves watching each other — man and beast — sizing each other up. Wondering. Curious. One of us afraid.

The dolphin's cries were continuous now — a steady, pulsating stream of high-pitched mews. They would stop briefly when I gently ran my fingers down its back and side — stroking that smooth, slick skin. Letting the animal know that there were others near. Others who would not hurt it.

Our veterinarian arrived, a man highly skilled in caring for distressed sea mammals. He checked the dolphin carefully and gave it a shot of antibiotics and steroids to combat stress and the infection that usually afflicts a beached dolphin.

Student staff members of the University of California's Moss Landing Marine Station near Santa Cruz were on the way to pick up the shiny blue beast and take it to their saltwater pool for study and further care. Our job until they arrived was to keep it wet and cool. And to let it know we cared.

Later as we loaded the dolphin onto a half-inflated rubber raft and into the back of a pickup truck, I felt a surprising twinge of remorse at not being able to go along and help. It is amazing that in a few short hours you can forge a bond of attachment with a creature you can't talk with. But sometimes just a look, the blending of two pulses in a touch, can be more powerful and can express more meaning than mere words.

By that evening, scientists at the marine

station decided the dolphin had recovered enough to be released. A contributing factor was the fact that the animal was stressed in the confines of a small pool and there was concern that it might injure itself. So it was taken seven miles offshore and released. It streaked rapidly away into the depths.

That was on a Monday. The following Friday the dolphin beached itself again 100 miles north, just beneath the Golden Gate Bridge. (A half-moon-shaped bite on its tail made the identification possible.) Members of the California Marine Mammal Rescue Center rescued my friend and took it to Marine World, where it is alive as of this writing.

Why did this animal go north to even colder waters, and then beach again? It seems to have pneumonia — at least they're treating it for that. But is that the explanation?

A week later we picked up another dolphin, this time one native to our waters, a Pacific white-sided, *Lagenorhynchus obliquidens*. And the next week another. Now Marine World has three of those intelligent sea beasts swimming in pools, similarly ailing and receiving treatment, looking toward their release as soon as they were well again.

Not all encounters between marine mammals and man are as mystifying as those with dolphins and whales can be. Last week we went out to help a distressed California sea lion found on another beach.

The animal was obviously weak, although weakness is relative when the weak one is 8 feet long and weighs in at around 300 pounds. There were wounds on its back; its eyes were crusty and half closed; and its sides heaved with the strain of just breathing. But when we approached, it immediately reared and showed its 2-inch canines.

When a distressed sea lion is in a location where you can't take a portable cage, the standard capture procedure is simple although sometimes a little insane. Two people approach with a net. The net is thrown over the sea lion, and one person adds a blanket so the animal can't see what's happening. The other person straddles the sea lion's back, grasps firmly behind the head, and pins the animal down so it can be rolled onto a lightweight stretcher and tied down for the trip to the vet.

This is definitely NOT recommended for amateurs! The first time I tried this I found that I could fly.

At the vet's, we discovered five bullet holes in the sea lion's flesh. The hapless animal did not live.

WILD BIRDS 2

No ladder needs the
bird but skies
To situate its wings,
Nor any leader's
grim baton
Arraigns it as
it sings.
— Emily Dickinson,
Poem (1883?)

GREETING THE DAWN like a golden eagle.

It was a typical autumn sunrise for the Diablo Valley. The low line of fat, rain-gorged clouds behind Danville had gone from pink to orange in a matter of minutes as the sun rose slowly over the tinted foothills.

Ching-Qualla, the orphaned golden eagle I was training for release, her tawny plumage blushing in the dawn, stood like a bronze Colossus, welded to her perch. Her eyes were on the skyline. She stared at each new phase of color, each new flicker as it vented its mood upon us, and even tipped her head to watch an instant airplane spark and die.

We stood there, close together, she all puffed and feathery warm and me in a nylon, down-stuffed coat. Our breaths mingled in the cold. Our eyes met, both reflecting color, and a feeling sparked between us as she tipped her head and chirped and briefly leaned against my arm.

Thinking back I remembered the time she'd stood teetering in her nest box, shakily towering over a young horned owl we were also raising — three times its size — regally, even then, letting it preen the feathers on her legs. And later gently returning the offering with a beak that could crush a rabbit's skull.

Or the times she chased the colored leaves . . . or caught and killed that funny piece of wool . . . or when I moved too close as she was eating and she grabbed my arm but didn't leave a mark . . . or that once she'd carefully preened my beard.

But now the sun was up and color faded from her cheeks. Her gentle eyes turned sharp amd searching through the grass, seeking out a ripple — checking for a flash of fur. I felt the pain of her anticipation as she closed her grip around my glove. Soon, she'd be free and making such decisions on her own.

And as we walked into the field, she cocked her head once more and checked a final fading cloud before the dawn.

WHICH CAME FIRST, THE CHICKEN OR THE EAGLE?

"**M**ighty Eagle Deplumed By Chicken," the story said. *"When the feathers cleared, a bald eagle, after attacking a barnyard rooster, was found to be suffering a broken wing and possible internal injuries. Farmworkers who rescued the bird and witnessed the fight said the eagle had been lucky to survive at all. The rooster was last seen strutting across the barnyard toward a group of cackling hens."*

"IMPOSSIBLE!" I roared, spitting coffee across the breakfast table.

"What is it this time, dear?" said my wife, dabbing at her housecoat.

"Only our Nation's Bird. Plucked from its last stronghold! Struck down in a pile of feathers!"

"What's a Nation's Bird, Dad?" peeped my son through his mouthful of cracked corn and other assorted seeds. I looked at him suspiciously.

"What are you insinuating?" I said, my voice rising.

"Dear!" clucked my wife. "It's a bad way to start the day."

Broken wing, phooey! I thought as I headed out the back door, muttering and pulling on my leather glove and hanging a bag of sliced meat over my shoulder. "Lucky to survive! Possible internal injuries!"

"Aren't you feeling well, dear?" the echo crowed behind me.

Once outside in the crisp dawn my head cleared and I felt a little better. Especially when I looked at my eagle. She greeted me with her usual neighbor-waking scream. I rubbed her beak on our favorite spot and stroked her wide, sensuously feathered back.

"How's my big, strong, brave eagle this morning?" I whispered, mentally comparing her massive hooked beak, the incredibly strong body, and the calloused feet, big as my hands, with curved 2-inch daggers . . . with the image of a scrawny white, skinny-legged leghorn.

Here I was getting ready to release this orphan back into the wilderness where she belonged, and suddenly, in one strutting instant, my faith in her ability to make it, my belief in her stubbornness to triumph over the second-rate teachings of her foster parent had been shaken to the core.

"Dear," cackled a voice from the back door. "It just said on the news that a story about an eagle getting beaten up by a chicken is believed to be a hoax."

The rising tide of relief made my knees tremble. "I knew it!"

I glanced down at the bird, meeting her innocent brown eyes. There was a spark, a brief flash of fire in those earthy depths. "I really knew it," I gritted firmly.

"CLUCK!" she replied, as if she'd known it all along.

Faith is believing what you know ain't so.
— Mark Twain

One summery day, I was standing just inside the front door of the museum, talking to Sam, the director. An early-morning coolness still lurked outside so we had a large fan in the doorway — sucking in some of that freshness.

Suddenly our conversation was interrupted by a loud buzzing sound, and two green imps materialized mere inches from our faces — in the earthly forms of a pair of young Anna's hummingbirds. They hung there quietly in formation, framed in the doorway, wavering like spots before our eyes. One of them moved so close its beak almost touched the tip of my nose.

There is nothing more curious and unafraid than a young hummingbird.

We stood there for a long moment, eyeball to eyeball, casually speculating as to what was on each other's minds. Then both birds pirouetted and tumbled down through the air in gentle cartwheels until they were almost flush against the back of the floor fan. They buzzed and hummed curiously about that fan, examining every crevice, probing every nook. Obviously looking for something. (I was dimly aware that the drone of the fan was not unlike the humming sound of their fantastic wings and I wondered aloud to Sam if the fan might not have called them to us.)

The inspection complete, they came up in front of us again, one zooming by Sam's face, one by mine. I slowly lifted my hand and stuck out my finger. That feathered flower purred in close, slowly, carefully, its needle beak extended; we gently touched; tip to tip in a tiny handshake.

Quickly, both were back in tight formation and *zooming* past us into the museum!

We caught up with them in the Reptile Room. They were dancing, wing in wing, from terrarium to terrarium. "Gee, a boa constrictor." "Catch those phony plastic flowers, Hector." "So *that's* what a rattlesnake looks like. Mom says they eat hummingbirds!" Another quick spin and they looped past our amazed faces and out the front door. Sam and I just stood and stared.

An hour later I happened to glance out the office door just in time to see an emerald green speck zip in through the front door, like the beam of a green flashlight peeping its way into the far, upper reaches of the museum.

I wondered for the next hour. Those little guys need to eat every 15 minutes and there is a lot of airspace in our museum; he could get lost and starve to death in a couple of hours.

Sybil calls up to say that our visitor is sitting on a ledge above her head, watching her clean some rabbit cages. (I tell her maybe he wants to help and she says at that rate it would take her a month to clean one cage.)

Zip . . . Peep . . . the other hummer comes power-diving through the door like a little jet fighter on full afterburners. Look-

A COUPLE OF HUM DINGERS dropped by for a visit.

ing for his wingmate.

Minutes later I slowly crept up on one of the little characters as he sat on top of a rabbit cage. As I close my hand carefully I hear a loud, irritated *peep!* Hummingbird swear words leak from my fist as I make for the door. My opening hand sets off a bright green explosion.

All the rest of that day, between phone calls and busy details, I worried about the other hummingbird. Somewhere, high in our rafters, he had to be almost out of fuel.

Late in the afternoon one of the museum aides spotted him, sitting on a beam with wings drooping in exhaustion. I cling, teeter, wobble my way along another narrow beam until I'm just below him; he watches tiredly as I scoop him gently onto my palm.

Down below Cheryl and McCurdy give him a stimulating drink of sugar and water. ("Thanks, I'll have another, barkeep.") Then, outside, a second green rocket follows the first into the yonder.

Can I ever be sure they weren't little alien spaceships sent down for their first visit to earth to view and study the natives? What had they thought about the critters living in our museum? The citizens of earth, as far as they were concerned.

And what are we to think of them?

I don't know about you, but for me, it's the little things in life that give it quality.

On New Year's Eve, a friend of mine in the wildlife rescue business took in an injured hummingbird at her clinic. It was a little male Anna's hummingbird . . . one of those fragile green jewels with the bright ruby throat that decorates your backyard feeders and winks you awake as you sit staring sleepily over your first cup of morning coffee.

The icy fog had left it lost and stiff with cold and its fruitless search for flowers had brought it close to death from starvation.

Hummingbirds are *hypothermic* — too much cold causes their body temperature to drop and they become dormant and cling to skinny branches until they die. Or sometimes they're lucky enough to catch a stray sunbeam long enough to get warmed up again.

But if they don't immediately find food, the demands of their high-energy bodies become too much and they crash to the ground and are lost forever deep in the noisy darkness of some grassy jungle.

We see a lot of them this time of year, and all wildlife rescue centers keep a little incubator heated up and waiting. If we get them in time, and shove their little beaks into an eyedropper of sugary nectar, they will suddenly burst back to life like the bud of a new flower.

My friend had a shoebox that was kept heated with three blue Christmas tree bulbs — blue so the light wouldn't hurt little

LITTLE THINGS MEAN A LOT, especially when they live.

eyes. She gently tucked the icy hummer under a Kleenex sheet and put the top back on the box. As soon as its body was warm, she would offer it a drop or two of energy.

And then my friend's phone rang. It was a little girl's father, wanting to know if the clinic helped something as small as a baby mouse.

My friend smiled as she glanced over at the shoebox.

They brought the mouse just at closing time — at 6 o'clock on New Year's Eve. God, it was a scraggly little thing. No bigger than the first joint of your little finger. Wet. Cold.

Like a miniature drowned rat.

It was late and my friend decided to take the mouse and the hummer home with her so she could keep an eye on them through the night. To save space, she dropped the shivering mouse into the shoebox.

At midnight her alarm went off. As you might have guessed, she wasn't big on New Year's parties, but as long as she had to get up to check her puny patients, she figured she might as well celebrate the coming of the new year at the same time.

She carefully lifted the top of the shoebox and peeked in. In the blue light of the Christmas bulbs, the hummingbird's scarlet neckfeathers were so intense they actually hurt her eyes. So it was a moment before she could see well enough to realize what was happening.

Then she spotted the tiny nose sticking out from under the warmth of the hummingbird's left wing.

In the distance, my friend could hear the sound of firecrackers as neighbors celebrated the new year.

But there, in the warmth of her bedroom, as she looked down into the cozy depths of the shoebox . . . there was nothing to be heard, except possibly the sound of two tiny hearts beating as one.

For some people that is more than enough.

*We never touch
but at points.*
— *Emerson*

BLACK THOUGHTS of an even blacker time.

As I walked into the museum the other morning I was suddenly aware of an odor that quickly sparked old memories. Not pleasant ones, either. Black ones.

It was the acrid reek of crude oil — the stink that makes people think of walking along old railroad tracks, or watching those hammer-shaped pumps endlessly chug up and down and up and down in the oil fields.

But I stopped having those kinds of associations during the great San Francisco Bay Oil Spill of 1971. For several weeks the days and nights were a shadowy black jumble of gooey, dark, stinking, glistening birds and raucous screams and plastic bags full of unmentionable dead things. That cloying stink of Oklahoma crude permeated everything. The oil formed inky lines under your nails. No matter how short or well-manicured.

Now, a glistening black apparition stood before me, teetering on the edge of a large, stained cardboard box. Every square inch of body surface, every single feather, everything right down to the shiny tip of its beak, was saturated with gooey stinking oil.

For one horrible moment I even entertained (bad word) the thought that this was not really a bird at all, that someone was playing a sick joke on me with a shiny piece of black plastic worked over with a blowtorch. But the smell was there. You can't duplicate that smell.

I wondered what the hell it was. Where from hell it was.

And then one eye slowly opened, painfully opened and hung there like a bright yellow moon in the dark, cold winter sky.

It was a great horned owl.

Three of us worked over that fearsome beast for the better part of an hour. A special soap worked wonders; the small injection we gave him made him not mind it so much.

He'll need another cleaning in a day or so when he gets his strength back, but I've brought him home with me and he's looking 1,000 percent better. He even looks like a great horned owl.

But I'll bet you're thinking, is one dumb, clumsy bird really worth it all? Three people, part of a morning's work, $10 to $15 worth of materials and drugs (at wholesale), more work and time to come. And even then maybe he'll die.

In that big San Francisco spill, more than 10,000 birds died, and here we dumb clucks are, slaving away over one dingbat owl that had the gall to get himself dunked in a private oil storage pond, one complete with NO TRESPASSING signs, yet!

As I sit here typing this, suddenly wondering what a big old owl is really worth, I look up and see those bright yellow eyes staring at me over the side of the box . . . and one of them slowly winks.

JUST ANOTHER DAY, as the lion went poo in his cage.

The other morning I got up and slumbered out of my bed and into the bathroom; I discovered four hungry fawns bleating in my shower.

I yawned, scratched my head with my little finger and mumbled off for the tub in the other bathroom. One musn't let these little impediments interfere with the start of an otherwise beautiful day.

Ruefully, there, I stared down at the arctic loon, hissing at me from my bathtub. Ah yes, I remembered distantly through the morning haze, you're from yesterday afternoon. It seemed like a year ago. Somebody shot a loon. So much for bath. I could feel a familiar stirring of frustration in my chest.

As I headed out the door for the kitchen and the blessed coffeepot, the loon's graceful movements sent ripples curling around my tub and caused the incoming tide to rise and fall against the dirty ring. Quaint.

I leaned against the kitchen sink, gasping as the cold porcelain hit my bare stomach, trying not to watch the foggy sides of the metal coffeepot as I waited for it to perk. The nervous drumming of my impatient fingers woke the five baby loggerhead shrikes and the two little orphaned house finches that had been snoozing in the incubators that lined the wall behind the sink. Damn!

"Honey?" came the barely understandable murmur of my wife's sleepy voice from the bedroom, "Can't you do something about your noisy birds?"

As I fed the little monsters, endlessly dropping piece after piece of food into the gaping bottomless chasms beneath their ever-groping little beaks, I glanced wistfully out the window at the beginning of a lovely, sunny day. A mother house finch was perched on the edge of her nest in the green of our kitchen-window shrub. Her youngsters looked quiet and well-fed. She was leaning back, her head tilted at an angle and her feathers slightly fluffed, soaking in the warm richness of that early sun.

Boy, I thought, birds really have it easy.

"Daddy," came my son's shriek from the back bedroom. "The lion cub went poo in his cage." Yeah, birds sure do have it easy.

When I got home from work that night, my dear wife met me at the door, alas. My wife *never* meets me at the door.

"Honey," she said., "Your daughter's having a slumber party tonight and they want to use our bedroom so they can all sleep in the big bed.

"Aw, darn," I complained. "You know I always like to sleep in the big bed. Where am I going to sleep?"

"I'll sleep in Corey's bed," answered my wife.

But that's a single and that means I'll have to sleep on . . . "

" . . . the couch," she grinned. "It's just for one night, silly. Stop fussing and help me feed the fawns."

"But the wolf cub sleeps on the couch."

Life is made up of sobs, sniffles, and smiles, with sniffles predominating.
— O. Henry ("The Gift of the Magi")

I clenched my teeth and imagined trying to sleep with that big wet tongue. I'd have to wear a raincoat.

Many reasons have been given down through the ages for a man's having to spend the night on the couch. But I don't think they can compare with: four fawns in his shower, a loon in his bathtub, a lion in his bedroom, and especially a giggle of slumber-partyers in his bed.

I wonder if there's a wildlife rescue center someplace that takes in distressed people?

RAGGEDY ANN flew high on tattered, lacy wings.

She bobbed there, barely astride the bucking wind above the ridge, her silhouette ragged in the dawn. She was like a broken kite that had been found by a child and taped back together without some of the parts.

Raggedy Ann was a red-tailed hawk — except that some of her russet tail was gone and her wings looked like the old worn-out keyboard of a honky tonk piano whose white keys might symbolize the empty spaces left by missing feathers. Who would have thought that any bird could actually fly with so many of its vital feathers lost?

I first met Raggedy Ann a year ago. She had come to the Monterey SPCA's Wildlife Rescue Center as a box full of bloody and broken parts that once upon a time had been a handsome bird. Limply she had come tumbling out of the sky when a hundred angry hornets zipped from the barrel of a shotgun to knock her from their deadly path. Her left wing had been broken and many of her feathers torn to shreds.

With our help, the wing bone healed in a few weeks. But the feathers were another story. It could take a year or more for them to moult and new ones to grow in. This is a very long time to keep a wild hawk captive — time for her to lose her wildness, or to suffer further damage in the confines of a cage. So we tried a centuries-old method of feather repair originated by falconers. You take the old moulted feathers of other red-tail hawks and glue them to the broken ones with wooden plugs. Since feather shafts are hollow, by carefully trimming and splicing — making sure you have a number two right primary feather tip to glue to the broken number two right primary feather stub still in the wing — you can create a sort of bionic bird. And when it's time for one of those repaired feathers to moult out, it still does, and a new feather can grow in to replace it.

IF, that is — IF the glue holds. IF the wooden plugs don't break under the stress of a flapping wing.

IF you have properly fitted tab A into slot B.

Repairs done, we took the bird miles away and cast her into the air. We held our collective breath as she climbed on those reconstructed wings.

Skill? Luck? Perhaps both. Not a feather fell.

Weeks later, something so unusual happened that I would not have believed it if I hadn't seen it. Raggedy Ann came back. Over miles of unmapped oak forest and scrubby canyons, she returned to a place she had come to only once before, and then by car in a darkened box. How did she manage to return, and why? What gave her the strength and drive to break from nature's normal ways and chase away a pair of red-tailed hawks that already lived here, so that she could make this place her home?

*The voice of Nature loudly cries,
And many a message from the skies,
That something in us never dies.
— Robert Burns (1759-1796)*

It has been more than eight months since Raggedy Ann came back to us. Many of the broken feathers we repaired have moulted and we are waiting anxiously for new ones to grow in. Meanwhile, her wings are still so full of holes it seems incredible she can fly. Yet as we stand and watch, she does — in elegant circles and graceful dives.

Her favorite perch looks down upon our hospital from the ridge. Sometimes when she flies low she stares down at us and screams. And we wonder what it is she says.

UP, UP, AND AWAAAY! in a barrage of bath towels.

Well, spring is here with a nice crisp shudder.

I knew it long before I found myself blowing steamy rings on the way to the car in the morning. I knew it last week, in fact, on the day the red-tailed hawk got loose in our museum. This is an Annual Event, you know; it happens every spring.

You'd have to take a look at our museum to understand my consternation at having *any* bird escape. Up there in that jungle-tangle of spidery metal rafters there's approximately 5,000 square feet of soaring space, and if loose red-tails have anything in common, it's that they like to soar.

This one — I'd already nicknamed him "Spring '77" — was no different from the others. When he arrived, we'd found a slight break in his outer right wing (from plowing into a car on the freeway when he swooped to nab a wayward jackrabbit). There was also some slight infection, so we put him in one of the special wards (boxes up on the mezzanine), and loaded him up with antibiotics, liquids, and food.

That was Friday. On Monday he was soaring.

I was just sore.

Let me digress a bit at this point, to clarify this situation . . . to lay the groundwork for your understanding of my inspired paranoia about this seemingly trivial matter. It's not trivial and it's no laughing matter — unless you count my hysterical giggles.

You see, Spring '77 isn't just any old bird. He's the sixth annual Spring Soarer since I've been here, with a couple of semi-annuals in between. And it's always been my duty (misfortune) to have to go up there and catch every last expletive deleted one of them!

That's the rub. You see, not only are the upper reaches of our museum long (100 feet), and wide (50 feet), they are also very high (50 feet). A loose hawk has a very large advantage over me, you might say. I can't fly.

Spring '76 was a loose vulture. (A real turkey, I think.) We were lucky with him. A platoon of 30 of our Junior Aides finally caught him in a spectacular barrage of knotted-up pastel bath towels — it was like the Fourth of July all over again — and it so undid him that he swooped down and landed on the carpeted floor and stood there begging to be captured.

Spring '75 and Spring '74 we don't talk about. Let's just say that both times someone managed to stop my headlong fall from the rafters at the last minute.

Spring '72 and Spring '73 were trapped in a manner that probably made Rube Goldberg roll over in his grave in astonishment.

With Spring '77 I decided to play it cool. This is, after all, the age of chemical warfare, of binary gases, luminous pesticides and buffered aspirin. So why not a little mickey in a mouse for a loose red-tail?

You never know what is enough unless you know what is more than enough.
— William Blake (1757-1827)

It almost seemed too easy. Thaw out a bunch of the frozen mice that we use for hawk food (insert here an appropriate joke on meat prices); inject mice with large quantity of acepromazine cocktail a-la-slee-pytime; place mice in strategic locations throughout the museum; wait.

It was that part about strategic locations that finally got me. They were 50 feet up and w-a-y out on some rickety 2-inch beams. Actually the beams themselves weren't that rickety. It was my legs.

Ten mice later, I was thinking about eating a few myself and taking a little nap until it was all over.

After three hours, the "starving" hawk hadn't touched a single medicated mouse. I huffed off home at that point, wishing that the bird would find and eat every mouse and hibernate until spring, at which point I would resign my job and let someone else catch him if he ever woke up.

That night, just on the chance that the bird's appetite might have improved with everyone gone, I snuck back to take a quick peek.

Now the first thing that meets your eye when you enter our museum is a series of large, glass-sided, top-opening cages that belong to our Pet Library Club. Inside the cage on your left are the guinea pigs. Inside the cage in the middle are the rabbits. And inside the one to the right are the white rats and a red-tailed hawk ... and a WHAT?

To this day we still don't know how he did it. It takes two hands (we've checked it out again and again) to open up one of those cage tops. But there he was, old Spring '77, standing in one corner of that rat cage with his crop stuffed so full of rat there was still the tip of a tail sticking out of the side of his beak. Jammed into a 4-inch-square section of the cage in the farthest corner opposite him were the other 40 rats that lived there, apoplectically goggle-eyed with dismay. (Perhaps that's not strong enough a word.)

And the cage top was closed.

Do I feel relief at his capture? Satisfaction that we saved another lost soul? Sympathy for the poor rats?

Actually all I can think of right now is, who's going to have to climb back up there and collect all those dopey little mice?

Does somebody smell something?

JOHN HAD A BABY, and guess who got to dice the mice.

We had anxiously been awaiting the hatching of John's and Julie's eggs; there was some good news and there was some bad news. The good news: They'd finally started to hatch the week before Christmas. The bad news: The first two hatchlings died.

John and Julie were two barn owls that lived on display at the museum where I worked. One day John laid an egg, and another egg, and another until she proudly nestled atop eight. At this point I'd better explain that John is a female barn owl and Julie is the male. (Oh, you noticed?) You see, it's sort of hard to tell the sex of barn owls until they do something like this.

The first hatching came as a surprise to us, even though we had been expecting it for weeks. (I guess this sort of thing is normal enough. Dad is never ready for Mom to wake him to go to the hospital.) When I slid my hand slowly under John's downy heating pad to check on all the eggs that morning, I discovered that one was all fuzzy and warmer than usual. My heart leaped clear into my throat.

All day I proudly watched and waited for John to feed her new-hatched chick. She'd sit there all motherly in her nest box, occasionally standing up to look down and wonder at her barely fuzzy child, sometimes nibbling at it ever so gently, allowing her beak to wander aimlessly over every line of its body as if to trace out the life that pulsed there.

But not once did she attempt to feed it.

That afternoon I tried to stimulate her into doing her job. Someone suggested that maybe the father should have been helping by handling the food and giving the mother pre-torn pieces of the more tender cuts of mouse. (He was snoring away in a corner of the cage the while, totally unconcerned.) So I knelt there next to her artificial nest, a pair of forceps in one hand, chopped mouse in the other.

There we were; me tearing up tempting morsels of mouse and John gratefully taking them, and eating them all herself. I was getting very concerned when, suddenly, she clasped a larger piece of meat in one foot, raised up her body by supporting herself with her wings, tore off a tiny piece from the hunk, tipped her head upside down so that her beak reached clear back under her soft breast, and started wagging her head back and forth as if saying no-no-no-no. All the time she stuttered softly, sounding like a broken record in mid-cluck.

The tiny blind chick, who had been lying behind a mountain of unhatched eggs, instantly raised its head at the clucking sound. With wings and legs and body all aflutter, it somehow wiggled straight for that wagging target of meat. Aha! Hooray!

My fists clenched in suspense and delight, then frustration, as I watched John swallow the meat just as the chick got in range, then carefully repeat those perfect,

Every beetle is a gazelle in the eyes of its mother.
— Moorish Proverb

wasted motions with an empty beak. I removed the chick to an incubator and took up the feeding job myself.

Three nights later, somewhere in the small hours, the incubator failed. The chick died when the temperature dropped below 72 degrees F.

John also refused to feed the second chick when it hatched. No way could I get her to even go through the procedure, though I tried all day and into the night. That night I again took her chick away. This time, however, I used an incubator with an alarm, in case something more went wrong.

Next day that chick ate greedily, strongly, actively. And come evening it suddenly drooped and faded in a frantic, bewildering hour. I'd probably left it too long with its mother. It's constant hunger, stimulated by John's clucking but unsatisfied for 24 hours, had probably fouled up its digestive system. And my providing food in plenty the next day was perhaps more than it could handle.

A convoluted way of saying I'd blown it.

How I dreaded the hatching of the third egg. I lay awake that night thinking about it. My stomach was a knot of uncertainty as over and over I thought through my next move.

The next morning it hatched. I decided to leave it under John and to assist her in feeding it while it was with her. This time we'd have a go at it together.

Every two or three hours I climbed into the cage and fed her, endlessly, those tiny bits of meat until she was finally stimulated into clucking and offering her empty beak to the chick. Then I would reach in and under her with my chrome-plated forceps and feed the chick as it responded to the feeding calls of its mother. That night was Christmas Eve.

At the end of the last feeding I weighed the chick. It tipped the scales at a mighty 20 grams. I left the usual pile of mice by the nest box for John's dinner and staggered home to my family.

The next morning, bright and early after Santa had laid out presents for the kids, I sneaked down to the museum to check and weigh the chick, to find out how much it had lost during the night.

It weighed 24 grams.

That was four grams *more* than it had weighed the night before!

That was the tiniest Christmas present ever given to me. And the most wondrous.

A SILVER LINING can also have its clouds.

You get to meet a lot of new friends in my line of work, but rarely are they as classy as Silver.

Silver is a good name for a bald eagle. On the surface it's a rather plain name, but it has the same simple elegance as the metal, and that really tells it like it is — or as he was.

Believe me, it's a shock seeing an adult bald eagle up close for the first time — and every other time, too, if you really want to know. Eagles may just be the most dramatic creatures in the whole English language.

Standing next to a bird that comes up to your waist is an eye-opener, but with bald eagles it's the beak that really gets your attention. That enormous yellow Excalibur dominates the whole bird. Accentuated by the pristine white of the head feathers, the beak suddenly appears from nowhere and curves out and down into a needle point, sinister and graceful and rich as an Aztec ceremonial dagger hammered of massy gold.

My first meeting with Silver, about four years ago, took place at the San Francisco Zoo, where a gentle man named Larry Coglin was training the bird to be released to the wild. It's no easy task to take an enormous bird like that, one that's spent uncounted days sitting on a slab-floored, steel-webbed cage, and teach him the even harsher realities of freedom. But Larry and a small team of dedicated people took on the job.

Seeing such a bird confined to a cage can do things to a person. It did something to Larry.

Silver had to be flown daily to strengthen those unused 7-foot wings. He had to be taken off his zoo diet of tasteless vitamins and ground-up incidentals and taught to tear at a more natural fare of large, whole fish. There was a lot more to it, but mostly it was time and flying.

It took two years for Larry to ready Silver for the wild, two years of two creatures working together and learning about each other. It took commitment and trust from both man and bird that some might find hard to comprehend.

Finally Silver was released at the Ruby Lake Wildlife Refuge near Elko, Nevada. Larry gave me a picture of that release that I will treasure always. It shows him launching Silver into the air. The great bird's wings reach for the sky with supernal, shining grace; the dynamic lines of man and bird cry out thunderously of striving and timeless freedom.

A year later I received news that a hunter shot and killed Silver, claiming he thought the bird was a jackrabbit.

Oh God! How could anyone think that?

You meet a lot of friends in our line of work, Larry's and mine.

But you lose a lot too.

The loving are the daring.
— Bayard Taylor ("The Song of the Camp")

51

BIRDS OF A FEATHER don't always flock together.

Picture, if you will, two enormous white pelicans. These cumbersome creatures can stand 4 feet tall, and they're very anthropomorphic. (That means with those big brown eyes and rubbery faces, they can get you very attached to them, like overgrown kids.)

Pelicans are totally unafraid of you when they're brought in for care. They'll wander around, poking those awful beaks into everything, picking your pockets, mingling with the staff like a bunch of interns out for their first lecture.

Picture these two pelicans as having received badly broken wings — multiple wing and shoulder fractures — so very bad that the birds will have to be put out of their misery.

Picture the doctor bending over one to give it that final painless injection. She looks up just in time to see the second pelican peering around the door frame with a curious look on its face to see what's going on.

The doctor, calloused veteran of many such deliveries, breaks into tears; someone else must euthanize the second pelican.

And so it goes . . .

GO AHEAD, MAKE MY DAY

One of our museum's volunteers, who shall remain forever nameless, was caring for a Virginia rail with a broken wing. (The rail is a little long-legged marshland bird about the size of a quail.)

Now what lifts an otherwise unremarkable story up out of the ordinary is the fact that this volunteer's husband is an ardent bird hunter. Complete with fully-trained bird dogs. Room for just a little conflict here, right folks?

Right! And the aviaries that hold the injured quail, ducks and rail that this woman is caring for are right next to her husband's dog runs. Getting the picture?

Well, the other day, as our heroine opened the aviary door to feed it, Mr. Rail zipped out and disappeared into her backyard. Panic and pandemonium!

She immediately rushes here and there and here again around the yard, looking for the injured but frisky rail, who can't fly but is something you wouldn't believe on those long legs. Its camouflage isn't bad either. When she calms down, she works out a search pattern and methodically goes all over the yard on her hands and knees.

Two hours later — green knees but no rail.

But our volunteers are creative. Struck with a sudden thought, she goes and gets her husband's championship Labrador, takes it out of its run and over to sniff around the rail's cage. Then she turns the dog loose in the yard with a command to "Search!"

Thirty seconds later the dog returns and gently deposits the unhurt rail into her hand. Nearly overcome with relief, she puts the rail back into the aviary. End of sequence.

Now all she has to do is keep a straight face when her husband comes home from his next hunting trip, complaining that the dog keeps bringing him rails.

Unless, of course, he reads this . . .

A MATTER OF PERSPECTIVE

Some time ago I was working to help raise and train a young orphaned golden eagle for release back into the wilds. She was one of the first eagles I'd ever handled and I was trying to develop a simple technique for rehabilitating this species.

We'd rise daily with the sun so as to be able to fly her before I had to get to work. Day after day of having sleepy eyes squint into the first glorious burst of the dawn. Day after day of lack of sleep, of tired legs plodding through stubbly fields until we could stir up a jackrabbit. Morning after morning of watching the pumping of those mighty wings as that awkward youngster tried, in vain, to catch those wily, speeding hares.

It was one of the most frustrating times of my life, as I recall. Getting that big bird to catch her jackrabbit, her normal prey, became the focus of my attempts to train her. If she could just catch a jackrabbit, I just knew that she'd make it on her own when freed. And if she couldn't . . .

And when it came at last, that day of days when her frantic wings whipped the air into a frenzy and she caught her first jack, I ran yelling towards her across the field, jumping up and down and tossing my stocking cap high into the air at this release of my long frustration.

That sounds pretty bloodthirsty, doesn't it? Well, that's a part of what I'm talking about.

Much later that same day, while I was back at work at the museum, a lady brought in a jackrabbit that had been hit by a car.

It had been cut up badly, and the wounds were deep and matted with dirt and tarry gravel. We worked long after closing time on that poor beast, cleaning out its many wounds, applying salves, picking out bits of gravel with forceps, bandaging where necessary, frequently giving it fluids and other medications to counteract the shock.

And then, just when we finished, it died. It quietly closed its eyes and let go a final breath, just when we thought it would live.

The next morning, while out flying the eagle, I thought about the jackrabbit that had died the night before . . .

JUST PLAIN WILD

Animals are such agreeable friends — they ask no questions, they pass no criticisms.
— George Eliot, Scenes of Clerical Life (1857)

A LIGHT TOUCH is needed to mend a butterfly's wing.

That such a thing as a butterfly can fly defies belief.

That such delicate thinness can best the boastful breeze, can bounce from flower to flower and can pause to sip the sugary nectar from each blossom is food for astonishment.

If you've nothing better to do than witness one of the world's great wonders, watch a butterfly. Become aware that movement, for the butterfly, is an infinite series of contradictions.

I was thinking these things, and more, as I sat on the grass staring at an orange-and-black marvel — a monarch butterfly. It was bobbing gently on a rose leaf. And one of its wings was broken. Like a crack in a Ming vase. Or wilted edges on a perfect rose.

I don't know when it was, as I sat there, that the idea came. But I know why. We owe a duty to such beauty, to repay the pleasure it gives us just by allowing us to look. I carefully broke the butterfly's rose-leaf perch from the stem, carried them both into my kitchen, and sat them down in the middle of the table. The butterfly didn't move, though the broken upper part of its wing banged against the bottom like a loose shutter.

The break was in the left wing, about a third of the way down. The top part of the wing was folded rather like the corner of a book page that someone had turned down. Flapping limply at the slightest movement, it was attached only by one of the thick black veins that crisscross butterfly wings,

strengthening them as did the struts and spars of an old-fashioned biplane.

I began to gather and sort my tools. I figured that everything I did would have to be guided by two rules — strength and lightness, each tied irreversibly to the other. I would need a brace, and a means of attaching it. But if it were too heavy (I wondered if a single drop of dew might not be too heavy) the butterfly would be overloaded on that side and unable to fly.

Glue was the obvious means of attaching my brace. I had some epoxy, and the tiny paintbrush I resurrected from a bottom drawer would help me apply the merest amount that would be needed for the job. But how to brace that gossamer wing? Every material I could think of would be like a steel beam welded to that fairy form. And those things I might think light enough would snap into a thousand pieces under the strain of those powerful wing strokes. Then I found myself staring at the bamboo shade on my patio. With my knife I sliced a hair-thin splinter from a bamboo strip. It was light, strong and perfect.

Actually it proved a simple procedure, as repairing broken butterfly wings goes. I painted the splinter with epoxy and waited until it was tacky — almost dry. Then with a pair of tweezers I carefully lifted the wing-tip back into position and pressed the bamboo brace against the black wing vein.

With the paintbrush I lightly brushed epoxy along both sides of the crease formed by the break in the wing. Then I sat still, holding the wing into position with the tweezers.

The butterfly trembled slightly from the shaking of my hands. After several minutes I breathed deeply and released the wing. It held. Except for the pale streak of bamboo along the black vein, the wing looked normal.

Then I thought, why hadn't I dyed the splinter black? I could feel myself starting to get the giggles. Picking up the rose leaf, I carried the butterfly back into my yard and held out my hand. Under the caress of a gentle breeze, the butterfly slowly moved both of its wings up and down, as if testing the air. The glue held.

Suddenly, the butterfly was airborne. Fluttering about my yard as if nothing had happened. Pausing to sample the nectar of a flower. Hovering to seek another. Rising upward on a warm draft of air to sail over my roof and away to some other garden.

I glanced down at my watch. Barely half an hour had passed since we'd met. I felt immensely refreshed.

Clumsy jesting
is no joke.
— Aesop
("The Ass and the
Lapdog")

Any business where you have to work with wild creatures is rife with pitfalls, but in the wildlife rescue business I sometimes think they should be more aptly called . . . pratfalls.

There are a million and one ways to get hurt in this work, and I don't mean just physically. There's also potential for embarrassment, shock, mortification, fear, and probably a few dozen more emotions that keep popping up at the most inopportune times. And even though the longer you are in this business, the more calluses you develop, you still never become entirely immune.

Oh, you can tell the professionals, all right. You know, the guy who always fights to hold the injured vulture so he can point it toward somebody else when it vomits. But that's not entirely foolproof as things can happen at either end of such creatures.

It's some of those unpredictable ends that I'd like to relate to you today, if for no other reason but to make you think twice about EVER getting involved in this insane work. A few names have been changed to protect the innocent, though I don't know why because there are NO innocents in this business.

One morning I was working with this extre-e-e-emely buxom lass. We were together as a team, cleaning cages. She'd hold the injured animal while I'd clean the cage, or vice versa.

I was bent down, merrily scrubbing away when I heard her let out a startled GASP! Looking up I immediately saw her problem.

The barn owl she was holding had grabbed her . . . er . . . uh . . . well . . . her buxomness. Funny it may seem as you read this, but not so very funny to the person on the receiving end of those four half-inch-long needle-tipped talons.

You think of the strangest things during times of stress. I remember thinking that at least one personal little mystery had been cleared up. There was no sound of escaping air.

There was only one solution, of course, and thank GOD we were alone. It didn't help when we both got the giggles, "God," she gasped. "I hope my husband never hears about this!" "Your husband?" I choked. "What about my wife?"

Along those same lines, one day a youthful volunteer came dashing into my office to say that one of our staff needed help with a python. From the look on his face I thought he meant HELP!, so I fell down the office stairs (it's faster) and ran into the kitchen where she had been feeding the giant snake. Lisa had the snake wrapped tightly around the upper part of her body . . . with its tail under her sweater, neatly peeling the garment up over her head.

"Dammit!" she screamed. "Will you get out of here! I said I needed help from a woman!"

"Sorry," I yelped. "The secretary will be

in in about an hour . . . ."

"Damn you . . . !"

And then there was the time one of our staff was wrestling with a very nasty little foot-long alligator that bit him on the finger, lacerating it severely. After tearing himself loose, he dropped the angry little beastie into the toilet of our one bathroom, while he headed for the office to try and stop the bleeding. (Any place in a time of need, right?)

A few minutes later you could hear the mortal screams of my boss, who always took his morning constitutional at about that time, rebounding throughout the entire building. Oh, well.

Then there was the time a 12-foot python got loose and lay like a fallen tree across the door to one room, and visitors kept stepping over the log until one lady happened to look down . . . or the time I brought the "Animal of the Week" onto KTVU's "Romper Room" show, and a desert tortoise defecated loudly and wetly in Miss Mary Ann's lap and all over the designer dress that a local dress shop loaned her for the show. (They did it LIVE in those days, folks, and Miss Mary Ann was so very ALIVE like you couldn't believe it!)

You know, it's been a long time since I've been back on that show.

ANTHROPOMORPHISM, the magic that links us all.

Sometimes, try as you might, it's impossible not to make certain comparisons between animals and people. A pure out-and-out case of the dreaded and deadly anthropomorphism disease. The giving of human characteristics to things not human.

This disease can be downright fatal to a scientist, causing him to be shunned forever by his colleagues. Think about it. How much credence would you give to the research of a scientist who thinks all St. Bernards look like his Aunt Martha? (Especially if he was a plastic surgeon?)

Personally I can feel for the guy. I have had recurring attacks of this affliction myself over the years. And it has done dreadful things to my own credibility when I'm wearing my scientist hat. (Though I must admit, it doesn't hurt me much when they let me out and chain me to my typewriter every morning.)

Oh, I've tried to fight off its effects. To see that deer over there as a *black-tailed deer* . . . and not as Bambi's father. To look upon that darting hummer as an *Anna's hummingbird* . . . and not as the flashing green jewel on a fairy's waving ring finger. But it's hard. Oh God, it's hard.

Those animals keep doing *things*. you know . . . THINGS! And what's a poor soul to do if he has even the *slightest* twinge of imagination?

Wait . . . let me show you. Let me describe a recent event pertinent to this subject. You think it over and YOU be the judge.

One of the birds most commonly treated at wildlife centers near the ocean is the cormorant. This is a lanky, black web-footed bird with a long neck and a long, wicked beak that lives in the ocean and dives after fish. The Japanese fishermen fasten long lines to their legs, put small rings around their necks so they can't swallow anything, and fish with them.

They stand about 2 feet tall and are mean beyond belief. If one comes in with a broken wing and we take him out of the box to try and repair the damage, he's bound and determined to take at least two of us with him.

So one day we get in one of those black devils with no apparent injury except for a clouded left eye. The vet says he's had those cataracts for some time and though he's almost blind in that eye, the other's fine and he's in perfect health.

OK, so sometimes animals get picked up by mistake for one reason or another, so we take him back down to the beach and toss him back. And when we park our truck in front of the hospital and get out, there's one of our animal control officers who's arrived just ahead of us, with a cormorant in a box. Said it was waddling down the freeway in the general direction of our center.

And it has a cloudy left eye.

So we throw him in the outdoor aviary with a few busted-up pelicans that are recuperating and decide to keep him for observation for a couple of days.

Two days later we release him again, only quite a ways down the coast this time. He didn't beat us back. It took him half a day.

Nine times we try to release this idiot. And nine times he returns. Sometimes he's found waddling doggedly down the freeway, causing us to get calls from the Highway Patrol. Sometimes he stands on the beach just below the wharf where all the tourists go, his head hung down, sighing loudly . . . until our phone rings off the hook from frantic people worried about the dying cormorant.

So one morning I arrive at work extra early, and happen to glance in the outdoor aviary. And there's old One-Eye, gurgling contentedly under the wing of a big old busty female pelican, making lovey little quacking sounds as only a love-struck, half-blind cormorant can.

Draw your own conclusions.

Gee, if I had more space, I could tell you about the two honeymooning pelicans that crash-landed in the back of a truckful of anchovies . . .

SAM was a cat who could make a wolf stand up and pee.

We've got this cat that thinks he's got some enormous power in his right paw. His name is Sam and he is an ordinary looking, run-of-the-mill, 12-pound, gray-and-white tomcat.

But at one time or another in his long life, Sam has put the fear of God into mountain lions, coyotes, eagles, bears, and most recently, into a certain arctic wolf I know.

So how does a housecat get to lord it over these fearsome predators, any of which could gobble him up in mid-lope?

Well, actually it's quite simple. I think. You see, Sam has always been in on things from the very beginning. When a 2-pound orphaned cougar came to our house, Sam was there to console it and play with it and reprimand it when it was a bad little lion. And since the lion grew up thinking old Sam was his father, why should anything change just because he got to be a little bigger than dear old Dad? Well, 10 times larger might be more than a "little bit," but in these matters, it's more a matter of attitude than of altitude. Big kids just don't usually talk back to their little fathers.

When Sam would get angry at one of his foster children, he'd simply raise The Paw and *bwap* them on the nose with a fistful of claws. They would yelp, screech, squawk, howl, or whimper off into a corner to lick their wounds and contemplate their sins.

As a rule, all Sam had to do after the first few days of this kind of training, was to raise that masterful Paw, and whether they be lion, wolf, coyote or bear, they immedi-ately stopped whatever they were doing and hit the deck. It got so bad with Mac, the young arctic wolf I mentioned (wolves being the most submissive of creatures in real life), that every time Sam would make his entrance into a room where Mac was, the wolf would stand at attention and pee. Urination in front of one's betters, you see, is a formal sign of submission in the wolf hierarchy. (Right after that, Mac became an outdoor wolf. He had started looking on all our family members as his betters and our rugs simply couldn't take it. Neither could my shoes.)

There was worse to come, a power trip for Sam. He started flaunting The Paw. Oh, he went slowly at first. He'd be sleeping on the foot of the bed and would suddenly raise The Paw on high. Without even opening his eyes. There would be instant scurrying sounds as furry bodies dove under the couch, behind pillows and beneath bookcases.

I suppose it was harmless in the beginning. Sam would lower his paw and purr happily. But as it is with most addictions, I knew it was bound to get out of hand sooner or later. And it did.

I was getting ready for work the other morning and happened to glance out the window. There was Sam, sleeping in his favorite spot on the front porch, basking in the early morning sun, and there was this mastiff trotting up the street, chewing on a mouthful of someone's morning papers.

You know the sort of dog I mean. One of those mammoth brown numbers with a monstrous fat head that prompts mothers to run out and grab their kids when it trots by with a mailbox in its mouth looking for someone to play fetch.

So anyway, before I can move, this *big* bull mastiff spots Sam and heads for him at a gallop, massive paws digging out clods of lawn the size of hubcaps. And Sam sleeps on, oblivious.

Now everything switches to slow-motion. The *big* bull mastiff, all slathering, toothy jaws, is inches from Sam's fragile head. Suddenly (Sam didn't even open his eyes, I swear), The Paw rises slowly into the air, each sharp claw exposed to twinkle in the sun, one by one. Plinkity, plinkity, plinkity, *plink!*

I stared in amazement as that terrified dog dashed, ran, fell, tumbled and rolled back down the street, screaming all the way like he'd just stuck his nose in a light socket.

Sam was, again, quietly asleep on the porch.

I exclaimed to my son Jeff, who had watched beside me. "Did you see what Sam did with his Paw? Man, oh man, what a Paw! Did you see that Paw?"

But answer came there none. Jeff, too, had taken off. Maybe he had an urgent errand. Maybe Sam's Paw is gaining over people.

Maybe I'll take off, myself.

DEER JOHN is a chamber pot of horrors.

I'm frequently asked what I feel is the most special thing about the little museum I work for. Is it the wildlife rescue project we run? Is it our tame wild display animals that you can touch? Well, I'll let you in on a little secret, heretofore known only to our staff.

It's the john.

That's right. Our museum's lavatory is about the most special spot I can think of in the whole building. And it isn't because Karen Kari painted it sunshine yellow a couple of years ago, making it so bright that you scream when you open the door, have to wear sunglasses just to wash your hands, and get sunburned checking your face in the mirror, either.

No, our little water closet is unique because, well, because it's there. Or to be more specific, because it's there when we need it.

You see, people find and bring us these funny "problems" all the time — a trunkful of bear cubs, or an angry 5-foot alligator in a rotten gunnysack, or a "dead" deer that wakes up and starts doing a *pas seul* around the museum office, while Jeanne, our secretary, files herself in the top drawer.

And when, with two hands, you suddenly find yourself with three hands full of squealing baby wild hog, and frantically cast about for a place to put it, what can you do?

Well, you can lock it in the can, that's what you can do.

Down through the years our little sanctum sanctorum has seen some lively action.

Who could ever forget the Bumper Goose? The Bumper Goose was a large and lanky Canadian honker that some of us used to see every morning when we were taking the Red Cross canoe class at the reservoir last fall. She always stood at the front end of the park ranger's truck, admiring herself in the shiny chrome bumper.

Anyway, she came into our wildlife hospital one day, too weak to stand and nearly dead from a fish hook she'd swallowed. So into the privy she goes while we arrange for an appointment at the vet's. And when Cheryl goes back to the bathroom to take her to the doctor, she finds ol' Bumper Goose has dragged her weary feathers across the bathroom tiles and is primping before her reflection in the chrome piping under the sink.

Ah yes, at any time of day or night, in spring, summer, winter or fall, what would ordinarily be your average, run-of-the-mill trip to the head can turn into something reminiscent of a new recruit's life-or-death dash through an Army obstacle course.

There's usually a sign on the washroom door alerting the unsuspecting staffer, cryptic little hurried-off notes in the barely readable hand of someone who thought they might get an arm chewed off if they took too long.

"DEER John," or "Keep door closed, OR ELSE!" or "Watch yourself — Something

ELSE Is," or "Wear Gloves," or "Protect yourself up to the knees!"

This is one restroom where you can get tired.

You've heard of a boy's room and a girl's room . . . this one is a chamber pot of horrors. Someone once remarked that it was the most explosive powder room in town.

Actually, in case you haven't already guessed it, in spite of the bother we rather enjoy it. I mean, where else can you play hopscotch with a rampaging baby tusker, look up and find yourself eyeball to beaktip with an eagle, or tiptoe past a sleeping fawn?

Not everything is perfect, however. One day we got in a whistling swan.

In case you've never toed the line with one of these gigantic birds, let me set the scene. I'm nearly 6 feet tall and this big bird stood almost to my chest. And that was before she even started reaching for my nose.

For eight hours she held us off.

Our frantic staff laid siege to that place like hungry heathens trying to storm the moat of a treasure castle. But sturdy and staunch she stood, 7-foot wings asunder, 3-foot neck extended like a threatening spear, powerful beak open, and sinister hissing filling our nervous ears.

We finally won — an enormously relieved victorious few (it was too late for some) — and when we found a new home for the swan things settled back to normal.

But if next year our museum budget should contain a request for a certain capital improvement item, I hope our city fathers will understand, and give it the consideration it so richly deserves.

One doesn't ask to go back to outhouses without good reason.

A REAL BIRDBRAIN, or the adventures of a dumb cluck.

Between the animals and the machines — well, they're out to get me.

The other night we'd finished dinner, put the kids to bed and tuned in my favorite TV program. All those good things after a long day at work.

So what happens now? "Daddy!"

Only it isn't a call for the well-known glass of water. Or one last "Goodnight." Nothing that simple.

My daughter says footsteps are walking on her ceiling.

In my day we weren't so creative. But daddies are daddies, so I go in for the token listen, tuck her back into bed, bend down for another kiss, and then we stare into each other's eyes as we listen to, well, to the footsteps on the ceiling.

As we stand there, my wife, son and daughter all talking (it's amazing the crowds one can draw with tiptoes on the ceiling), I glance at my watch. Five minutes into my TV program.

"Come on you guys," I mutter. "Just a mouse. I'll check it out in the morning."

"No, Dad," interjected my infernally knowledgeable son. "It's the baby starlings. They nest in the side of the house over Corey's room. They must have fallen into the attic."

"So we'll let them spend the night there. It's warm. I'll put them back in the morning."

"D-a-d-dy!" chorused my wife, son and daughter.

Warm wasn't the word for how hot it was up there in the attic, as I chinned myself up through the black crawl-hole. Have you ever noticed how household stepladders are never tall enough to do you any good?

The flashlight fell out of my back pocket as I tried to swing my feet up.

I finally made it, holding the darn light in my mouth. As I pulled myself into the attic feet first I nearly swallowed it. I remember thinking that the surgeon wouldn't have any trouble finding it if the D-cells held out. I wondered if the company still did those advertisements about how their flashlight batteries saved people who'd been trapped in attics for days because they'd swallowed their flashlights.

There were two baby starlings. Their nest was a mass of straw piled against a vent hole under the eaves. The little birds had tumbled over the high backside of the nest and were skittering back and forth across the ceiling between two beams. All I had to do was crawl along one of the beams and toss them back into their nest.

Why do they always use beams with splinters when they build attics? What's wrong with using finished planks with nice smooth sides?

And why, when we all know that birds are going to build nests in the vent holes, do they design houses with roofs that angle down to narrow areas right at the vent holes? And why do spiders always spin webs in attics? In my whole life I've never seen a single fly in an attic. You'd think that when you were sweaty that the webs wouldn't stick to you. Wouldn't you?

Otherwise things went pretty smoothly.

Until the mother starling started pecking me on the nose when I plopped her youngsters back into the nest. She probably didn't want them back.

On my way back down into the house I leaned on the plasterboard trapdoor and broke off the corner and sprinkled plaster all over the rug.

"Honey! Darn you!" moaned my wife.

"Daddy! You're getting big black fingerprints all over the ceiling!"

I still had a half-hour left to my TV program when I'd finished vacuuming the rug. Just as I flopped on the bed, the TV gave a flash that dwindled down into a bright little bead in the middle of the screen.

"It's been doing that all week, dear," murmured my wife from her book. She tapped her foot on the bed and the screen lit up again with the last 20 minutes of my favorite program.

I settled back to watch with a sigh, scratching my dog's head as she lay on the bed beside me.

So the TV blinked off . . . on . . . off . . . on . . . off . . . as the dog's wagging tail thumped rhythmically against the bed.

A happy dog . . .

PART **II**

And That's What Life Is All About

THE BEASTS

For every man the world is as fresh as it was at the first day, and as full of untold novelties for him who has the eyes to see them.
— Thomas Huxley,
A Liberal Education (1868)

ANITA AND ARABELLA, the world's first space spiders.

Spiders have always held a special fascination, but spider interest rose to new heights a few years back when two of them shot into space on the U.S. Skylab satellite. With a good deal of pomp, Arabella and Anita blasted off on equal footing with the astronauts. The men wore shiny suits and glass helmets; the spiders, clear plastic vials. (Well, almost equal footing. One assumes that the astronauts wanted to go. Volunteered, even. I'm not sure that can be said for the spiders.)

The reason for taking these arachnids along: Arabella and Anita were of a kind, the orb spinners, noted for their ability to spin strikingly beautiful, perfectly round webs. You know the webs; you frequently see them stretched across a corner of your hedge, sparkling like halos, woven of dew and glory by early morning's sun. Our scientists wanted to know how zero-gravity would affect the web-making. (Think of all the ways mankind could be saved by that fine datum!)

Only Arabella attempted a web, and she didn't do too well. Floating in her slick, 6-inch-square, clear plastic, geometrically engineered cubicle, with nothing to hang onto, she just couldn't get it together. I'll bet the slide rules did slide and the computers did bubble at this strange inability of the eight-legged earthling to adjust in space, especially when compared to her two-legged companions and their own eager overadaptations.

Picture the overworked computer throwing out handfuls of ticker-tape answers . . . MAN . . . IS . . . SUPERIOR . . . TO . . . THE . . . THE . . . SPIDER . . . and the delighted little grins of the scientists as they read and passed along the word to the President.

Anita never spun a web at all. She floated morosely in a corner of her artificial bush until she died.

Originally there had been no plan to bring them back alive, but the public response, when they found out about the spiders, was overwhelming. PUBLICITY . . . IS . . . GOOD . . . FOR . . . THE . . . THE . . . SPACE PROGRAM. So NASA decided to bring them down again and study their ability to readapt on earth. Only they ran out of food. (Weight is a critical factor in a spaceship. TAKE . . . ONLY . . . TWO . . . FLIES . . . FOR . . . EACH . . . EACH . . . SPIDER.)

One of the astronauts offered to donate a drop of his own blood, brave fellow, but the computers opted to feed the starving arachnids on a leaner diet of rehydrated bits of freeze-dried steak, just like all the other crew members. For some reason the spiders didn't like it. A rain of confetti fell from the computers . . . IT . . . DOES . . . NOT . . . NOT . . . COMPUTE . . .

Arabella died on the way down.

It was announced that the remains of the spiders would be studied to find out what had happened. Days and weeks and dollars must have been spent weaving delicately detailed theories, and hours of valuable computer time consumed in tracing the causes of the final effect: THE . . . SPIDERS . . . ARE . . . ARE . . . ARE . . . DEAD . . .

But maybe they were looking just a little too hard for the answers. Why should we expect a spider to spin a web where flies cannot fly? And what happens to a spider's instincts when there are no twigs to anchor its web, nor dew to coolly wet its strands? How can a mere spider face the enormity of having to spin its web round and round the entire world?

Dear scientists, faithful computers, when you took up your microscalpels to carve away Arabella's last mortal remains, did you bother to check her heart?

You may have found it broken.

Winnie the shrew could paralyze a giant potato bug with a single blow to the midsection. And he often did.

Winnie the shrew was so-o-o fast, he could sneak away while you were blinking your eyes and be back again before you even noticed.

When Winnie the shrew was hungry he could inhale more food for lunch than you could eat in a whole week, and he would still be ravenous before dinnertime. Could you eat your own weight in food every day? It did not even give Winnie gas. But the most amazing thing of all about Winnie the shrew is that he was only three-fourths of an inch long. He could climb right up on a quarter and slide down George's nose.

When I first met Winnie, he was hiding under an oak leaf on the bottom of a peanut butter jar. A lady had found him that morning when the cat dragged its irate prize, kicking and screaming, through the cat door into her kitchen. The cat accidently dropped the shrew at that point and immediately backed, hissing and spitting, against the refrigerator. Winnie had his hypodermic-needle teeth sunk up to the hilt in that little pink spot just under one of the cat's claws. He was hanging on for dear life while pussy played handball with his body on the linoleum.

Right off, the lady figured with those moves it couldn't be a mouse. So she climbed down off the kitchen chair and scooped Winnie up in the peanut butter jar.

I told her she had been pretty lucky to

WINNIE THE SHREW lurks in toe-level jungles.

catch him. He had probably been getting ready to finish off the cat and didn't see her coming. That is when the lady screamed, "Oh my God, the cat!" and turned and ran out of my office.

And that is how Winnie the shrew came into my possession.

I looked down at the jar and wondered how strong it was. I also wondered what had happened to her cat. I have a delicious imagination.

I hoped the shrew had not been in the jar for too long because shrews have such a hyper-metabolism they can starve to death in a couple of hours without food. I carefully opened the lid just a crack, thinking even a crack might be too far for a shrew, and quickly dropped in an earthworm I happened to have on my desk. (Don't ask.) Winnie caught the worm before it hit bottom. Then I watched fascinated, as Winnie's slender, pointy grey-brown snout jabbed out from under the oak leaf. It began twitching and working on one end of the worm like a hungry kid on a piece of spaghetti.

Winnie was an ornate shrew, *orex ornatus*, a species of mammal — an insectivore — that is among the smallest of warm-blooded predators to prowl the toe-level jungles of the world. His not-so-distant cousin, the pygmy shrew, is so small (with no other mammal smaller) he could get exercised doing laps around your fingernail. Hard to believe, isn't it?

To find these little guys you have got to be willing to meet them on their own level. But that is stooping pretty far.

Not much is known about the personal habits of these magical mini-mammals. Oh, we know that they have a super-high metabolism, that their little hearts beat a couple of hundred times a minute, and that they grow old and die after six or eight months or so of this fast-paced living. Because of their continuous need for food we also know that Mama Nature has made them absolutely fearless of the giant prehistoric insects on which they feed.

They are not afraid of cats, either. Unfortunately for them, an oversized ego is not enough to help a shrew come out on top in a fight with a monster cat.

Winnie was pretty lucky. The nice lady had probably saved him from getting his pea-brain scrambled when she caught him in that jar. Cats never forgive toe-biters. As it was, one of Winnie's little legs stuck out at an angle and she figured it was broken.

But what do we really know about them? About how they live out their insanely flickering little silent-movie lives? What can you say about an animal whose whole world might be the 6-foot strip of flowers in front of your house? You cannot even find his tracks so you can follow and see where he goes. Footprints do not show on a grain of sand.

Overcome with curiosity, I prepared a 5-gallon aquarium for Winnie and placed it on top of a file cabinet in my office. His right front paw was indeed broken. But it was much too small to set (the cast would weigh more than his body) and I was afraid to release him in that condition. To live out his kind of adventuresome life and survive, he had to be in tip-top condition.

I landscaped the bottom of the tank with hills and valleys of sand and earth. Twigs lay scattered about like fallen redwoods, and a fist-sized hunk of lava towered above one end of the valley like a miniature Annapurna.

As an afterthought I dropped in the oak leaf he had been hiding under in his jar. The lid from a ketchup bottle rounded things out as a picturesque little lake. (OK, so you had to see it.)

Winnie the shrew proved to be quite a fastidious little fellow. He dug out one cave under his oak leaf as a cozy sleeping area. In another he stored his surplus food. He nipped his crickets on the back of the neck, paralyzing them so they stayed fresh for an hour or so until his demanding little body needed their nourishing juices. Another cave, far from all the others, served as his tiny bathroom.

Winnie honeycombed his entire world with little trails, pathways among the fallen redwoods that he could use for a scenic stroll along the banks of the lake. Walkways up the back of the mountain, where he could stand and view the whole valley.

Sometimes I got the spray bottle and made it rain and he would run excitedly in 50-cent circles and rub his body against the downed trees and clean his sensitive whiskers with his paws and scrape his chin on the edge of the ketchup bottle lid. In short, he would have a gay old time.

During the time I had him, I think Winnie grew a little. A 16th of an inch, more or less. It's kind of hard to judge. Those things can slip by you when you're not looking. But he did get fatter, and his grey-brown coat was shiny and thick.

Living was easy for him with the steady supply of crickets and mealworms and the stray spidery treat I sometimes slipped him. Every couple of weeks I would catch him in the old peanut butter jar and screw on the lid while I remodeled his little ecosystem. For days afterward he would explore each miniscule crevice and dig out his new living quarters with a tiny blast of sand. Final-ly he would fire up his musk glands and stink up the place until everything was just right.

One morning Winnie the shrew did not come out for his morning cricket. After half a day I became concerned and gently lifted the oak leaf roof from his private sleeping chamber. There was old Winnie, still curled up in his favorite sleeping position. Dead of old age after five months of the good life.

I buried him by the redwood tree in my back yard, under his dried oak leaf. He didn't need much room. I just stuck my thumb in the soft earth, and he made a perfect fit.

SNAKES I HAVE KNOWN AND LOVED, especially Stanley.

Every year at this time when St. Patrick's Day slithers around, I get kind of introspective because I'm reminded of all the snakes I've known and loved over the years.

It all started out in a little five-room farmhouse in Agra, Okla., where I spent a lot of time with my grandparents when I was a kid. My first memory of a snake was the poisonous copperhead my grandmother was chopping up with the hoe.

My grandmother had absolutely no prejudices as far as snakes were concerned. She chopped them *all* up with a hoe. You'd think that basic training would have kept me from developing any longlasting reptilian relationships.

It didn't.

By the time I was 10, my room was full of cages and my mom lifted the covers with a stick when she vacuumed under my bed.

My dear old mom was amazingly understanding about these things. She even gave me a 5-foot boa constrictor one Christmas. "My son is a good boy," she'd smile. "Just stay out of his room."

Even when my pet watersnake, "Torpedo," oozed out of the heater vent and plopped into the middle of her ladies' club meeting, my mom kept her cool. She just dropped Torpedo in the toilet and invited all the ladies into the kitchen for a drink or two until I got home.

It took me 10 years to work up enough nerve to ask her what 49 women were doing singing "Ninety-Nine Bottles of Beer on the Wall" at the tops of their lungs in our tiny kitchen when I arrived from school.

Over the years since then, I've become acquainted with thousands of snakes. Everything from South American anacondas, to Cape cobras, to tiny worm snakes. But every year when March 17 approaches, three of those snakes invariably come to mind.

The first — "Sweetie Pie" — was a 14-foot reticulated python that belonged to one of the reptile curators when I was working as head curator at the Lindsay Museum in Walnut Creek. He used to bring the huge 150-pound reptile to work with him and she'd lie around the museum looking like a tree trunk.

That was all well and good until a Brownie troop came through on a guided tour one day. They all decided to sit down on the "log" while they were listening to the tour-leader explain how snakes take advantage of their markings to camouflage themselves when they're stalking their prey.

What can I say? In her own primitive way, Sweetie Pie was probably very hurt when the Brownies suddenly "evacuated" the room after she started nuzzling one of the mothers on the arm. Heck, she was just a very affectionate snake.

For the life of me I can't remember the name of my second favorite snake. All I can remember is that she was a 6-foot boa who was going to help me teach a class on

"How Not to be Afraid of Snakes."

For weeks I'd advertised the class in all the local media, and more than 30 people had paid $25 each to attend so they could lose their snake phobia. On the night of the class, that unnamed constrictor (bless her giving heart) and I sat there in front of the empty rows of chairs . . . waiting . . . waiting . . . for those people to arrive.

After three hours it finally dawned on me that they were all too scared to come learn how not to be frightened by snakes. With a sigh, I gave the disappointed boa a hug and returned her to her cage with an extra mouse for her troubles.

I never met a snake I didn't like, but if I had to pick a favorite, I'd pick a laidback western rattlesnake named "Stanley."

Stanley's claim to fame, if you want to call it that, is that he was a Hell's Angel. He was the mascot of a local chapter of that infamous motorcycle club and prospective members had to reach into the jar that contained Stanley and scratch him on the head.

If they survived, they could join.

Stanley was a member in good standing until the day he accidently nipped the club's president on the thumb and almost sent him down into Hell's Angel Heaven. When he recovered, the club gave Stanley a motorcycle escort over to the the museum and donated him to the reptile collection for "educational purposes."

I guess they decided to use a safer method to welcome new members into their club in the future. Maybe running the gauntlet, or swallowing a live hand grenade.

Stanley has been living at the museum ever since, maybe 15 or 16 years now, and you'd never know he was a former Hell's Angel just to look at him. Thousands of school children parade past his cage every year, learning that rattlesnakes aren't the fearsome ogre's that legend makes them out to be.

I guess that's what makes Stanley so special in my mind this St. Partrick's Day.

Despite his macho past, he's just one of the guys.

FAIRY TALE FILLINGS in soft, downy nests.

The hummingbird lives with the elves, and they stuff their nests with fairy tale fillings.

Have you ever watched a mother hummingbird build her nest? Now's the time, though I warn you, you may end up with a crick in your neck and you won't find any gold in a hollow stump. But, if I may be so presumptuous, there are still other treasures to behold.

The next time you see a hummingbird, watch it. Follow it with your eyes . . . your body . . . your feet . . . your mind. You may be lucky. It may be building a nest. If it's not, no loss.

A newborn hummer is a delicate thing to behold and the mother must prepare for its coming with great care. When most birds build a nest they use the normal makings — string, straw, strips of cloth, hair. Their young are lusty, hearty . . . and large.

A newborn hummingbird the size of your little fingernail (if you are a small person) is another story. A fairy tale.

The mother, like a tiny tinsel Tinkerbell, dances around each tree, daintily gathering the tattered remains of cast-off wispy cobwebs. Carrying this gossamer cordage all bunched up in her slender beak like a fuzzy halo, she pirouettes and hovers here and there and here again. There's just nothing softer, you know, than old cobwebs.

Next she collects the freshest, softest lichens and mosses with the expertise of a graduate student in botany — carefully selecting and fitting them into the tailored, silken moulding of her cradle.

The final touch — the lining — she saves as her own as she pulls and tucks in the softest of her breast down. And what is softer than one's self?

All of this is cradled on the end of the gentlest of bobbing branches for the wind to sing them to sleep. Is it any wonder that they only drink from flowers?

Great engines turn on small pivots.
— English Proverb

THE DESERT NIGHT brings out the best.

We hunched around a quiet spring in the Death Valley twilight, silhouetted against moonlit jagged peaks like some strange nighttime cacti spawned by the full moon's rays.

The silence was stirred suddenly by a soft clop, clop, clop: wild burros in a long file were picking their way along a trail to the desert spring. We could just maybe make out their shadows now, 15 long-eared, fat-nosed, high-rumped ghosts . . . no, 16. One shadow hung far back to the rear.

"That's the 100-yard burro," Bert whispered loudly in my ear, reading my mind. "That fellow doesn't get along too well with the old boy who's boss. There's a boss in every herd."

The kids are excited now. I can feel it in the air. This is the culmination of the whole trip. We've been out a week — traveling high desert trails across Nevada and California, painting the land with our eyes, tasting the crisp, chewable air, cringing and flinching from the awesome stroboscopic concerts of desert thunderstorms. We've run madly, wildly into desert whirlwinds. We've watched a horned lizard eating a spicy dinner of ants, a rattlesnake crawling across the road (to get to the other side, of course!), and a hummingbird feeding on a cactus flower.

We've eaten together around the dusty chuckwagon, and seen the world in a whole new light around the campfire.

And dreamed the heady dream of stars.

And now we wait, silently, tensely, eager to share another desert secret — the visitors to its water holes.

We hear the big brown bats drinking from the spring in front of us. They whirl and dip and dive around our silent heads like bobbing butterfly shadows left over from the sunny afternoon.

We feel them breeze about our heads, feasting on the mosquitoes we've attracted. I wonder if the kids are thinking of the old tales of how bats get tangled in your hair.

The lead burro stops; tall, proud, uncertain. I can see his nostrils flaring darkly in the moonlight as he seeks out the subtle odors. Is something lurking at his spring?

Five, 10, 15 minutes he stands, cast in bronze, never once looking at the water that he must thirst for so much. Nothing moves but those searching, soft, hungry nostrils.

And his power over his herd is such that none of the others dare pass him to reach the water. Even a tiny, unknowing youngster stands unmoving, unwobbling, at his mother's still knee.

Finally, the night sends a little stray breeze across our backs — one sniff becomes a ponderous snort, becomes a sudden billow of dust.

The burros plod back along the way they had come, stately, unannoyed at our intrusion, simply content to be as patient as the land.

A FLIGHT ON THE WILD SIDE with some fun-loving vultures.

There's a ridge high on Mount Diablo where the wind pours out across the saddle like floodwaters over the quivering lip of a straining dam.

And this is where all the turkey vultures gather to play.

Like sunburnt youths, their red heads glinting in the bright sunlight, they paddle around in the lazy quiet eddies above the oak trees, bobbing together like a group of surfers waiting hungrily for the next big wave to crest and break.

One suddenly eases away from the pack, slipping sideways through the air, breast feathers nearly scraping a sprawling buckeye-shaped reef as its wingtips quickly stroke faster, faster, faster . . . propelling it downward along the curving line of the ridge until it is just inches above the ground and sliding straight into the middle of the saddle where the fast-moving current gushed out across the canyon in an icy, breezy spray.

When the lone vulture reached the center of the ridge where it curved down to its lowest point, the full force of the wind as it rushed down the side of the mountain and was channeled through the saddle, struck the great bird on its right side at a 90-degree angle.

With perfect timing, the vulture rose high on the feathertips of one long black wing and pirouetted gracefully, sharply, around to the left and was immediately launched down and out and up into the waiting universe with breathtaking speed until there was nothing but a black speck against the sun.

And then just the hot, bright sun.

And then just the glowing red sparks that are left when you close your eyes against the glare.

I laugh to myself, wondering at the startled thoughts of an astronaut as he looked out the window of the space shuttle and saw a turkey vulture keeping pace with his craft high above the Sea of Galilee.

It's as if that first solitary vulture was testing the waters for all the rest, and found them perfect.

All barriers are suddenly down and it's every bird for itself as they jostle and maneuver against each other for the best positions.

One after another the big black carrion eaters peel off down the side of the mountain and are blown out across the canyons in a spew of black feathers. Wobbly paper gliders, spiraling, banking, turning ever upward from the blowing force of the mountain's breath.

And when the ride is over, they return again and again throughout the afternoon, bumping wings like little kids lined up for a turn to swing out on the end of a rope and fall into the swimming hole below.

Do animals ever play?

Do they participate together in games?

Do they find fun things to do in their

When I'm playful I use the meridians of longitude and parallels of latitude for a seine, and drag the Atlantic Ocean for whales. I scratch my head with the lightening and purr myself to sleep with the thunder.
— Mark Twain (Life on the Mississippi)

environmental playgrounds . . . just for the sheer pleasure of doing them?

Do they enjoy the very act of just being alive?

You don't have to ask. Just go for a walk and look up and see for yourself.

Late in the day as I stroll slowly back along the ridge, watching the last of the afternoon revelers glide off into the hazy distance, I am suddenly caught in a grasp of wind so strong I'm almost tumbled off the mountain.

As I spread my arms to catch my balance, I couldn't help but wonder what it would be like to be able to mount the prancing winds across the canyon.

The thought is almost too tempting for me to resist. But I fight it.

This time.

But one day . . . .

A CHRISTMAS GOOSE
brings us a tasty Christmas treat.

Do you believe in Santa Claus? Let me tell you what happened to my family last Christmas.

The phone call came late in the afternoon on the Sunday before Christmas. A couple of guys, fishing at a local reservoir, had found an injured bird. Could they bring it by the museum for care? Sure, I told them.

My 14-year-old daughter and I had to drive down to the museum anyway. The museum was closed, but that's where my wife's presents were stashed; Corey was going along to help me wrap them.

Two young men were waiting at the front door. The bird was wrapped in a large towel and bundled under one arm, but the head and neck were uncovered; two bright black eyes quietly observed our every move.

"Daddy!" Corey exclaimed. "A Christmas goose!"

She was right. It was an enormous Canada goose . . . one of those great gray-and-black honkers that wander across the crisp winter skies in endless searching V's.

As she lay there on the office counter her eyes were even with mine. With her large head level and unmoving, supported by a 15-inch neck, the problem quickly became apparent. With an effort I broke away from our staring match and looked down.

Wound around the base of her neck was a heavy tangle of fishing line. She'd obviously not realized it when she became ensnared, and had kept on eating until her esophagus above the cord had become swollen and packed with food.

Now she was weak. So weak that she couldn't fly or even stand. She could only sit, with her 3-foot wings folded silently, gently along her back. Those intelligent, all-knowing eyes stared deep into my own, daring me to help.

She made no move to use her powerful beak when I reached out to probe that fat, ugly pouch. It was as if an obscene growth had taken over a foot-long stretch of her throat.

Cutting away the cord was the easy part. Clearing out the packed food without causing further injury was going to be the problem. In the meantime, the two young men had to leave; we parted with mutual thanks and a "Merry Christmas!"

While Corey stood by our goose, I phoned the museum's veterinarian and filled him in. "A Christmas goose?" he chuckled. "It figures!"

The choice was harshly simple. If the bird was strong and fat, we could attempt to add water and break up the mass in her throat so it could pass along through her digestive system. That would be slow, but safe. If the bird was weak (as he spoke I saw her head start to sag on the end of a suddenly tired neck, as if to answer his question), if she lacked enough body fat to

Blessed be childhood, which brings down something of heaven into the midst of our rough earthliness.
— Henri Frederic Amiel, Journal, Jan. 26, 1868

carry her for several days (her breastbone, once I could locate it under those super-thick feathers, was as sharply defined as a knife), if it was an emergency — then the procedure would be to make a small slit in the neck, into the distended esophagus, and physically remove the material.

It was Sunday. Precious time would be lost if the vet drove to his hospital. A long ride to meet him there would further stress the rapidly fading bird. So I thanked him over the phone for his advice. He wished us the best of luck (especially the goose), and a "Very Merry Christmas!"

I looked at my daughter. We were both suddenly alone, suddenly very close together. "Ever read about Florence Nightingale in school?" I said.

Her eyes darted to the goose's, then back to mine. Then they got very large. She nodded.

We used the large sink in the intensive care section of our tiny wildlife hospital. It's so small that if you turn your back to the sink, you're immediately in a recovery ward, staring (at that moment) at a cross-eyed mockingbird that was recovering from a skull fracture.

Corey held the goose by both wings; the bird was suddenly so weak that her head sagged limply to the sink bottom. Her eyes started to close. No time to waste from here on.

Pinch an area clear of feathers, a quick swipe of ugly-yellow antiseptic soap (why am I cleaning off the outside with all that filth inside?). Easy now, snip a slit across the surface of that great, doughy mass below her chin — God, what if it explodes?

The bird was so spaced out she didn't even feel it. I didn't hit any major vessels so there was very little blood, but as I bent closer to make sure, I was almost overcome by the powerful odor of black swamp mud. Geese feed on the grasses that grow on the bottom of the bay and this one was full of grass and what smelled like a goodly portion of the bay bottom as well.

It had been packed there for God knows how long, and was completely dried out. The flushing technique would never have worked. Nothing was going to work except to chip away at that gooey, black adobe.

Half-way through I glanced sideways at my daughter. "OK, hon?" She nodded, then turned her eyes again to look back at the wall. Her face was white but her hands were still holding tight to the great bird's silent wings. I had never felt so close to my daughter.

Finally, after several acorns, a bay seed the size of a large marble, and a last pungent pinch of water weed, we were through. We put a clean bandage around the goose's neck like a bit of white silk ribbon around a special Christmas package.

With Corey still holding the bird, I quickly passed a long plastic tube down that long throat and gave her a cool, life-bringing draft of food and water.

By the time we three got home, that all-knowing head was again perched atop the sturdy neck, those sparkling black eyes were again meeting ours, matching each concerned glance with an equal gleam of confidence.

And would you believe what my wife and son were doing when we arrived? They were watching "The Miracle on 34th Street" on TV — that wonderful old classic about the department store Santa who claims to be the genuine Kris Kringle.

And so it came to pass that we named our Christmas goose "Kris." And we cared for her in a special "gift-wrapped" box in a quiet corner behind the pile of Christmas packages by the tree. Her life was a priceless gift for us all.

Our family welcomed the New Year together by releasing our Christmas goose at dawn on New Year's Day. Arm-in-arm we watched her disappear into the early morning sun. And if anyone ever asks, our entire family still believes in Santa Claus.

And this Christmas, when children strain their ears for the jingle of sleighbells and the patter of tiny hooves on the roof . . .

All of us, no matter how much older we may have grown, or where we might be, will be listening for the faint honk of a high-flying Christmas goose.

(The following is dedicated to mother mice everywhere, especially on Christmas Eve.)

A CHRISTMAS STORY
dedicated to mother mice everywhere.

The little grey mouse lay there on her stomach, panting, gasping, her sides heaving up and down under the terrible strain.

She was fat, not with the fat of food but with the gift of child, or in her case children — the fat of life. The fat of the land.

She lived in the hollow walls of a large house, in a nest made of rug nibbles and chewed-up pieces of the morning news. Outside it was frosty cold and hazy with rain. Inside, where the people lived, it was toasty and a bit warm.

In between the walls where the little mouse lived, it was just right.

It was nearing her time. She groaned — yes, even a mouse can do that — and her eyes squeezed tightly shut. Her fat little sides pulsed with the living rhythm of new life fighting to escape its confines.

She gave birth to nine this night of nights.

The efforts and pain of her actions was almost more than she could stand . . . but there was no hesitation . . . and finally, beside her . . . entangled in carpet swaddling . . . was a squirming little handful of nine, blind, hairless, rosy little mice.

Inside the mother was an emptyness she had not known for 16 long, lonely days and nights. Now there was just the limp exhaustion, and a little glow that only a mother could really understand.

It was evening now, and all was stark and still. Outside the frost was forming in little sparks on the grass. Inside, the fire crackled softly and reflected warmly from the little red stockings hanging on the mantle.

On top of the little fir tree was a small glass star that twinkled brightly and lighted the way to a little hole that had been gnawed beneath the bookcase. And there, in the comfortable darkness in between, it shown down upon the tiny nativity scene.

The mother mouse lay stretched atop the nine little babes, her eyes closed, her body asleep and unmoving, except for nine tiny pulses on her breasts.

And again, like maybe once upon a time, a long time ago . . .
*"Twas the night before Christmas,
and all through the house,
not a creature was stirring,
not even a . . . "*

THE CRAZINESS 2

Life is a pill which none of us can bear to swallow without gilding.
— *Samuel Johnson (1786)*

A WHALE OF A SONG, heard around the world.

Something very exciting has been announced in the field of animal intelligence. Something with such far-reaching implications that it is impossible to predict just where it might all lead.

Scientists have discovered an animal species that composes music on a par with humans. In fact, their songs are so complex and beautiful, and continually changing, that they compare with the best human composers such as Beethoven.

Honest! This was announced in January 1980 to startled scientists at the American Association for the Advancement of Science Conference in San Francisco, by Katherine Payne of the prestigious New York Zoological Society.

You don't believe it? Read on. Payne and her husband Roger have analyzed more than 600 songs by these incredible animals. And from this research, the Paynes and their colleagues have learned:

● The animals adhere worldwide to a form for their compositions (just think about *that* for a bit).

● They constantly alter the rhythm, pitch, and timing of their haunting music; each new song is so directly derived from a previous song that the next improvisation can be accurately predicted.

● Each single note is a unit, and a song involves a group of repeated units, with each repeat considered a phrase. All phrases of one kind make up a theme; there are from eight to 10 themes in each song. (Sound familiar music teachers?)

● The number of phrases in each theme changes, but the sequence of themes in any song is always the same. A remarkable feat of memory, since these creatures continue from one song to another without pause, sometimes singing for an hour or more.

● All creatures from a particular area sing the same song and all immediately learn the newest tunes from each other. ("They're absolutely always up on the newest, hottest thing," Payne was quoted as saying.)

● These animals use a technique much like a human composer's to create beautiful and interesting music. Payne, who trained as a musician earlier in her academic career, further commented, "For example, Beethoven sets up rhythmic patterns and musical themes we all recognize and expect to recur. Then he surprises us with a variation. Every one of these animal songs surprises me just the way Beethoven did."

The researchers exclaim they still have no idea what all these songs mean, or why they are changed so often, but they suspect the music has to do with courtship, aggression, feeding patterns, and social position. If I didn't know better I'd think they were describing some of our human songs. Certainly a classic human-courtship song could be Elvis singing "Love Me Tender." We start getting into the other aspects of human lovelife with "Do You Think I'm

Sexy?" by Rod Stewart. Aggression might be the National Anthem sung by 50,000 Houston Oiler fans. Feeding patterns? How about, "If I Knew You Were Coming I'd Have Baked A Cake?" And social patterns is, of course, "Hail to the Chief."

Wouldn't you suspect that such gifted creatures would also be able to communicate with one another on a high level — and maybe with other creatures too? We attach our own human labels to their sounds, calling it "music." After more research into the matter, might not the Paynes be calling it "language?" When words leave off, music begins.

Food for thought, you must admit. In any event, it is certainly exciting that we have finally discovered another creature that seems to have an intelligence comparable to our own.

You know, ever since I was a kid I always wondered how we'd treat another species if we found it to be intelligent.

But I didn't think we'd kill them and feed them to our pet dogs.

Poor whales. No wonder humpbacks sing such sad and lonely songs.

A WINTER DAY in the life of a loggerhead shrike.

Fog. Mother Nature's breath on a frosty day.

There's a crusty old loggerhead shrike wintering over in my yard. Every morning I see him outlined in the fog, standing out in the bare-boned bushes like a last leaf that refuses to fall.

Loggerhead shrike. A predator of insects, small reptiles, birds and rodents.

A stocky gray and black bird the size of a large robin with a black mask across the eyes as if to keep it from being identified when it leaves the scene of the crime. The sharply hooked tip of its beak is perfectly designed for killing. Its call is harsh and grating to the ear.

In the Midwest they call them "butcher birds." If there's anything left after they've eaten their fill of a kill, they tear off pieces and stick them on rose bush thorns or tuck them in cracks in the bark. The meat dries into sort of a natural jerky that the shrike can come back and eat later. It's also food for ants and other birds that may be lucky enough to find it.

As it is with all predators in the wild, surplus food never goes to waste.

We always think of scrub jays as the brash bullies of birdland, but the loggerhead shrike is the pro. Intimidation is his game and he plays it tirelessly, inventing new ploys and subtle nuances in the name of dominance.

My old shrike shares his territory with a pair of idiotic scrub jays. I think that's why he stays here. Those two jerks never catch on to his sly schemes and provide him (and me) with endless entertainment in between his occasional hunting forays.

Our favorite game is a sort of feathery "King of the Hill." It's diabolically simple. Every time one of the jays lands on a branch, the shrike flutters over to land on the same spot and the jay moves, barely one step ahead of those sharp talons. The jay is easily as large and strong as the shrike, but the intense willpower is missing.

The shrike will stay with one of the jays for two or three minutes at a time, hopscotching from branch to branch, up and down and back and forth and side to side and up and down again. And then suddenly, just as the totally frustrated jay is ready to blast off for parts unknown, the perceptive shrike zooms straight for the branch where the other scrub jay is sitting and the game has a new player.

The jays never seem to get wise to these Machiavellian maneuvers, and I've glanced out the window 45 minutes later to note the game was still in progress.

This morning, along with the fog there was a brisk wind. It sliced through my beard with an icy blade that sent shivers down under my thick wool sweater to remind me of my vulnerability.

Such a wind has a way of toying with you to help keep things in perspective.

I looked up and saw the shrike. It was sitting on the highest, most exposed branch in the shrubbery, facing directly into the wind as if to challenge it to penetrate the downy armorplate that encases its body.

The wind responded with a rush that ruffled the shrike's breast feathers and brought a smile to my face.

I moved, and the shrike turned its head and our eyes met.

I wondered if it was tempted to fly down to duel with me for the spot where I was standing. And if it did, I wondered if I would move.

But after a moment the shrike turned once more into the wind, so I wandered off into the fog.

Last New Year's Day my family was invited to make the annual "Trek To The Tree."

TREK TO THE TREE to watch another year pass.

Friends of ours live nearby, at the base of a ridge that is part of a long, low range of hills across the valley from Mount Diablo. At the very top of those soft-looking mounds just above our friends' house, stands a peculiar oak. It looks, in the distance, like a miniature green geyser spurting life up from deep beneath the earth.

Some time ago, perhaps after a New Year's Eve adorned in incredible revelry that extended far into the morning hours, we first hiked up to that lonely tree. Since then the hike has become a symbol of the change that takes place from one year to the other. With that tough climb to the top, as the cold winter winds sponge the perspiration from your face, comes soul's cleansing. A chance to change. To start anew.

Cold going we had of it last year, very cold. The wind fingered through our clothing and raised goosebumps on our arms as we started out in mid-afternoon. But after the first 100 yards we were so warmed to our task that we didn't notice. We whistled up the trail like a line of little locomotives, steam puffing from our mouths. (I think I can, I-think-I-can, IthinkIcan . . . can!)

My son and daughter, the youngest of the party, were so energized that they dashed about us, back and forth, like a brace of sheepdogs chivvying a flock of old and obdurate sheep. They doubled, I'm sure, the distance they had to climb, but somehow, always, they ended up ahead of us in the distance, waiting. "Come on you guys! What's keeping you?"

Eventually, we debouched from the tree-line, closed ranks and marched out onto the velvet green carpets of the first ridge, and I sighted the hawk. She hung there effortlessly, not far above us, like a mobile in the crisp air. And alongside her — of equal size — hung the moon, icy white and full.

Together they seemed to symbolize the change that was taking place within us as we moved up the hill. The moon: ancient, old, pale as death, wise beyond everything but past comprehending the year we'd just finished. The hawk: young, resplendent in her warm coat of feathers tinged with the rich brown of new earth; young eyes feasting eagerly on everything that moved or stood below.

Then, as we knelt beneath her, she tucked her wings and dove out across the valley until she merged with the distance, with the houses and cars and poles and lawns and bridges and land and water and people.

On the hilltop, the last bit of afternoon was warming our tree. It was a powerful spot, a powerful moment. All of the winds of the valley were also gathered there, and they swirled about and fluffed the branches and prepared it for the night.

My rosy-cheeked son came running,

blowing up to me, the tattered remains of a yellow plastic kite clenched in his hands. "Look, Dad," he puffed. "Somebody lost their kite and the wind tore it up."

He threw it into the air and dashed off down the ridge, dragging it along by the last bit of string. But it crumpled lifelessly to the ground and bounced along upside down behind him until finally even the string broke.

"No," I whispered to the wind as I stood looking back down the way we had come. "Nobody lost their kite. That's just the old year lying where it fell last night."

I raised my eyes out across the valley, where the hawk had gone.

"Ah, Jane, come with me to the tree house!"
— *Tarzan of the Apes*

When's the last time you tried building a tree house?

Last weekend I started building my first one. Ever.

We've recently moved into a new home, and right outside the family room window is an ancient, gnarled weeping willow tree ... a gigantic, many-splendored thing that covers the whole side of my house like an old-fashioned, humpbacked Mary Poppins umbrella with dangly, weepy, willowy branches. As soon as I saw it, as soon as my son saw it, we both knew "that'd make a neat tree house!"

I firmly believe that every man has, deep within him, an urge to build a tree house. It's some primeval spark that he is born with, that's kindled when he watches his first Tarzan movie ("Ah, Jane, come with me to the tree house ... "), and it starts to smoke when he first escapes with Tom Sawyer, Huck Finn, or Salinger, until it blazes into full, sun-garnished glory when he finds the right tree.

We had a double-handful of nails, No. 7, galvanized. One can't be too careful in recording his first tree house. We also had some 2x4's, wide planks of assorted size, hammer, saw ... hummmm, what else? Well, besides me and my son, what else did we really need?

Somehow I had the feeling that we could have done without nails, wood, hammer and saw, as long as we were doing it together, and as long as we had the tree.

Together we crawled out along the biggest limb. Me in front, scooting carefully along on all fours like I'd once seen an old raccoon do. Jeff walked along with the safe unconcern of youth, until we reached that one wide spot where the tree had decided we ought to build.

I placed the first board carefully, ceremoniously sighted and centered the nail and handed that golden hammer to my eager son. He raised it ... paused.

"Won't the nail hurt the tree, Dad?" his eager face was suddenly concerned.

"Well ... yes and no," I said. Why do they always ask you things like that when you're not ready? After some thought, after looking up through the branches as they rippled like shoulder-length hair being combed by the wind, I answered.

"I don't think it'll hurt the tree, I mean with pain like us. What we have to be careful with is not to make a lot of cuts and holes where the insects, or a disease can get through the protective bark and hurt the living tree inside."

I sighed, my balloon suddenly filled for the first time with uncertainties, doubt. "We ... you also have to realize that the tree won't look the same when we build on the house ... "

He sat there, silent for the moment, as he stared up through the living, moving branches. "Maybe we should just build a little place, Dad."

A scrub jay settled on a limb just a few

MY FIRST TREE HOUSE
never really got off the ground.

feet away, squatted and cocked a shiny eye at a cat in the grass below him, then with that first startling BANG! BANG! BANG! of my hammer the bird became suddenly aware of his new neighbors.

He launched into the air, commenting hoarsely on our presence, significance, heritage, and anything else he could think of.

A mockingbird, attracted by the commotion, landed about us and glanced sharply about as he sought the reason for the jay's anger. His accusing *tich! tich! tich!* hovered above us like a shaking finger, bawling us out for being so high up, so out of place.

I was suddenly aware of the wind hissing around us in pulsating waves, bringing the angry murmur of the crowd; the rhythmic bobbing of the tree, up and down and up and down, like the time I first rode a boat under the Golden Gate and into the sea; the pressure of my son against my arm as we unconsciously pressed together in embarrassment.

Tomorrow, maybe, we'll see about that second board.

THE GIFT came wrapped in a fluffy package.

The youngster carefully settled himself behind the living room couch, pulling the blanket over his shoulders against the cool, dark hours ahead. He had removed a bowl of flowers from the coffee table to clear his view of the large, empty fireplace. Tonight . . . this Christmas Eve . . . he was going to do it for sure.

An hour later, his breath came slowly and evenly. The blanket made a toasty pocket where he had laid his cheek — just for a minute — and fallen gently to sleep.

A long time later, maybe about 3 a.m., he woke to a soft scraping sound in the fireplace. His heart pounded. He pulled the blanket tighter around him to muffle its thumps. It must be Santa! He was climbing down!

Unable to contain his excitement, the boy scaled the couch, slowly, slowly tiptoed around the coffee table and carefully moved the fire screen. Just as he knelt to peer up the chimney, an extra loud scrape and a black puff of soot brought something tumbling into the fireplace before him!

The boy fell backwards against the coffee table, frantically pawing at the soot in his eyes to see what had dropped. There it was: In a back corner of the fireplace two bright yellow eyes blinked from a coal-black lump.

Creeping closer, the boy saw a tiny bird, a little owl. It opened its smudge of a beak for a thin, quavering call . . . *who-o-o-o-AH-o-o-o-o-AH-o-o-o!*

When he reached out to touch it, the little owl made sharp, snapping sounds and fell on its back, menacing with teeny, sharp-toed feet.

The boy retreated, thought, then unhooked a red flannel stocking from the mantle; he dropped it carefully over the struggling bird. Cupping the sooty ball of fluff in the stocking, the lad stood staring in the dim light. The yellow eyes stared back. The boy wondered what he should do.

Finally, he went to the front door and opened it, awkwardly, with half a hand. Pausing in the doorway, he smiled at the miniature owl.

"Merry Christmas," he whispered, and opened his hands to the night sky. With three silent wing-flaps, maybe four, the owl vanished, leaving a puff of black dust and maybe another little cry.

Moments later, the young man crouched again behind the couch, awaiting Santa.

Soon he was once more fast asleep, never guessing that for him, Saint Nicholas had already arrived, that he had held him in his hands. The boy had been left with a gift far greater than he knew, one that would live with him always.

HOLD THAT TIGER, and stuff him back in his trunk.

My friend gave me a tigerskin rug the other day.

She had this enormous, ancient skin all carefully rolled up in an ornate wooden steamer trunk in her garage. It was one of those old teak trunks into which people used to pack their lives. The skin had been lying in it for years, passed down through the family from once-upon-a-time when someone was a missionary in Asia.

I felt a tremendous conflict in this gentleperson as far as the tigerskin was concerned. She's deeply involved in caring for orphaned creatures of all shapes and furry callings until they are old enough to get back into the wild. To her, the skin of any wild creature — especially one taken as a trophy on which to wipe one's egotistical feet — is the very essence of offensiveness.

Yet this tigerskin rug had been passed on to her down through her family, and her family ties were strong. The rug was a vital connection with a long-lost loved one, a little last link to memories of another time.

You can't sell something like that. You can't destroy it. But you can give it to a friend.

Enter my own emotions. As she creaked open that dusty trunk lid in the flickering twilight of the garage, I felt hair start to rise on the back of my neck. I could actually smell the musty incense, hear the spellmaker's leathery chanting.

It was a classic old tigerskin rug — body, legs and tail all tanned and stretched out flat on thick black felt, the head mounted with eyes and mouth open in a lifelike pose. It'd been rolled into a bundle, to squeeze the enormous creature into the denlike trunk. The head, as in life, was propped alertly on top.

The expression was one of unrestrained fury. That taxidermist had really known his business. He'd probably even killed a tiger. How else could he have so excellently copied that look of utter hatred?

The ears lay back flat on the pumpkin-sized head. Its jack-o'-lantern mouth snarled wide, showing sharp, 3-inch fangs that had bitten with such force when the animal was alive. They were now cracked and yellow.

When she'd offered me the skin, my first reaction was one of instant, horrified rejection. After years of working with mountain lions — raising them in a lifelong experiment to return them to the wild; loving them; losing one in an unnecessary death — I could think of nothing more abhorrent than a tigerskin rug.

And yet . . . I felt something stirring deep within. A latent desire? Some ancestral need? Some subverted fascination? (Let him cast the first stone that is without . . .)

Even now I'm not sure why I accepted it.

My thought (my excuse?) was to put it in my den, its den, with a plain white marker asking: WHY IS THIS CREATURE DEAD? Food for thought when my

There is no object on earth which cannot be looked at with a cosmic point of view.
— Dostoevsky

friends came for a visit. A source of endless conversation and debate with the unbelievers.

As I lifted it from that mystical trunk and brushed against the whiskers — they plunked like the untuned strings of a sitar.

It was dark when I got home. The rest of my family was out shopping.

The cat had been untold years in that trunk, and she stretched out lithely across my carpet with a lash of her tail, with her meathook claws forever poised and ready at my feet. Those bright orange stripes had faded with age to match the teeth, and her head had a horrible death-grey splotch that ran back along the shoulders. I had never seen anything like it on a live tiger.

Why is this creature dead? I thought.

When my family arrived from the store, my son, the youngest, summed up all their feelings: "Oh, Dad . . . "

"Why was it killed, Daddy?" whispered my daughter.

On the next day I met my friend again. "I don't think we'll be keeping that tigerskin rug of yours," I said.

"I understand," she consoled me with a wistful smile, unsurprised. She sighed.

"Just put her back in her trunk if I'm not at home."

SNAKES ALIVE, that thing is really BIG!

Don't ever underestimate the power of an inflatable rubber snake.

Danville's Mrs. Smith doesn't. Neither does her husband, nor her gardener, nor the courageous animal control officer from the Animal Services Department.

By the way, "Smith" isn't her real name. I've decided to change it for obvious reasons. I know that her husband, her gardener and a certain courageous animal control officer will understand immediately.

It all started last week when Mrs. Smith discovered she had a problem. Her plums were ripe and luscious and the birds were eating them faster than she could pick them. So she stopped by a local plant nursery to see if they had any suggestions and immediately became enamored of a collection of lifelike 6-foot inflatable rubber snakes that are guaranteed to scare the living daylights out of any birds that decide to drop by for a snack in your plum trees.

So she buys one and takes it home and blows it up. While she's doing this, her husband is taking a peaceful nap on the couch.

Mrs. Smith takes the now gigantic serpent out into the back yard and attempts to drape it realistically over the plum tree's lower branches, but she can't reach high enough. Not wanting to disturb her husband's snooze, she coils it on the lawn at the base of the tree and goes shopping, fig-uring he'll be up when she gets back and she can get him to do it then.

Oh yes, he'll definitely be up before she gets back.

Not long after she's gone, Mr. Smith is awakened by the sound of the gardener hammering on the back door. Excitedly, the man explains about the monster in the back yard.

Mr. Smith gets his binoculars and checks it out from the back porch and agrees that this is indeed a frighteningly large reptile for one to find coiled in his back yard. So frightening, in fact, that it is now time to call the Animal Services Department for assistance.

After hearing Mr. Smith's description, the dispatcher immediately sends the first available officer to the scene. There are many poisonous reptile species being kept as pets (illegally) throughout the Bay Area, and one never wants to take chances.

Upon arrival, the officer takes one look at the sinister serpent (handy things, those binoculars) and decides it's much to big to fit in his gunny sack, so he goes back to his truck for his "come-along." (This is a 6-foot-long metal pole with a noose on one end that is normally used for restraining angry pit bull terriers, rabid bears and escaped gorillas.)

While Mr. Smith and his gardener watch from a safe distance with the binoculars, the brave animal control officer sneaks around behind the great beast, eases his noose over the bulbuous head and . . .

Life imitates art far more than art imitates life.
— Oscar Wilde,
The Decay of Living
(1891)

99

YANK!

When Mrs. Smith gets home and discovers what's happened, in between hysterical outbursts of laughter, she tells her husband, "I'll bet you all died laughing!"

"It wasn't funny," he responds, icily.

"Where's my rubber snake?" she asks.

"The officer took it to the pound," he replies, smiling.

So Mrs. Smith phones and tells them she wants her snake back.

"That will be $10 bail," they answer.

"But it only cost me $5 in the first place!" she pleads.

"We're sorry," they reply. "But we had to dispatch an officer to get it, so there'll be a $10 fine to get it back."

"Forget it," she snickers. "Just the thought of those three grown men trying to catch a rubber balloon is worth it! By the way, am I required to vaccinate it, too?"

(NOTE: *Secretaries at the Animal Services Department would be wise to open all desk drawers verrry carefully for the next week or so.*)

GUEST APPEARANCE on TV with Grandfather Nature.

I received a late evening phone call from a local gentleman who produces shows for small Bay Area TV stations. He had a problem.

He had this Saturday morning kids' show about animals and ecology and nature (whew!). The show's sponsor, Marine World/Africa USA, was supposed to provide animals and trainers for the show. Hence his problem. The show was being taped early the next morning and through some mixup . . . no animals.

He wanted to borrow some of the animals from our museum for the show.

"It'll be no problem," he said. "It's a real simple format. We've got this little African village, and everything happens on the grass in front of this little native hut."

"But we don't have any African animals . . ."

"No problem," he answered. "We'll have some little American visitors and Grandfather Nature can talk about their big African cousins."

"Grandfather Nature . . . ?"

"Yeah!" he chortled. "Great concept, right? Come on, it'll all be over in an hour and we'll even give your little museum a plug."

The thought of our "little museum" supplying animals for Marine World/Africa USA was simply too much to pass up. "Well . . . OK," I sighed.

"Great!" he yelped. "We'll put you on right after the Swahili lesson."

That cinched it!

I took my assistant Dave along to help with the animals. Also John, the barn owl, Willis the short-eared owl, a couple of European ferrets, and a tarantula. The studio was down near the San Francisco stockyards.

"I can't believe it," said Dave, holding both hands over his nose.

As we sat there watching them prepare the set, three pretty secretaries cooed over our little animals, while we cooed over the pretty, blonde Africa USA animal trainer in the tight blue hot pants. "A barn owl?" she said in a dazed voice. "But where are my lions?"

"I can't believe it," whispered Dave.

"The lions or the hot pants," I whispered back.

"Whadda ya MEAN, there's NO script?" raged the director, as the producer attempted to explain that we had some new animals that weren't in the old script, thereby making the old script useless.

"OK," smirked the director, evilly. "Emergencies like this are what a well-coordinated team like ours is for. We'll all work together. No one person carries the load . . . cameramen point your cameras . . . I'll stop the show at 10 after, 15 after, and 25 after for the commercials . . . and Grandfather Nature can fake it on everything in between."

"I really can't believe it," whispered Dave.

A difference of taste in jokes is a great strain on the affections.
— George Eliot ("Daniel Deronda")

Then Grandfather Nature walked onto stage center. He had a bright green cossack shirt with puffy sleeves and a Chinese collar . . . tight cowboy pants with bell-bottoms . . . shiny lizardskin boots . . . and eyebrow pencil marks all around his mustache to make it bigger and darker.

"Where's my toucan?" he said as he squatted on the log in front of the African hut and looked at the owls. "Those aren't toucans." He picked up one of the ferrets. "And where the hell are my lions?" You could see in his eyes that the whole scene was gradually slipping from his grasp.

"Fake it, Grandfather . . . " grinned the director. "Fake it . . . "

The ferret defecated in his hand.

"I can't believe it," whispered Dave.

The producer rushed over to me and pleaded. "You've got to go on with him and help him talk about these animals. He doesn't know a thing about owls and ferrets . . . just toucans and lions. Please . . . "

I could hear Grandfather Nature's quavering voice in the background, starting the show. "Jumbo, children. Ecology is everyone living together . . . "

"Sure," I whispered to the producer, as I lifted the giant black tarantula from his cage and headed into the hot sun of the African village. "I'll be glad to help. After all, it's not nice to fool with Grandfather Nature."

"I can believe that," whispered Dave.

THE ELEMENTS AND THE LAND 3

For many years I was self-appointed inspector of snowstorms and rainstorms, and did my duty faithfully, though I never received one cent for it.
— Thoreau (1817-1862)

HEAD OVER HEELS IN LOVE and filled with wild thoughts.

Once upon a time, before the dawn, in fact, I insolently dangled my legs over the edge of a 3,000-foot granite cliff, and stared off through the misty nothing air across an endless league of Nevada desert.

The air is so pure, scrubbed to its atoms by a thunderous bath the evening before, that I feel I can see forever. Like if I barely strain, I can even look into the future. Maybe just beyond that last, faint blue range I can discern the glimmer of tomorrow's coals, banked and made ready to light a new day's sun.

I am somewhere in the desolate White Mountains of Southeastern California at the 12,000-foot level, I guess, give or take an eternity. It is earliest morning with the sun not up, only its glow. And I myself have just awakened from the kind of peaceful sleep that can only come from such closeness to the heavens.

Yesterday's thundershowers still darken the skies to the northeast, looking like black marble all roiling and alive with changing veins of sharp white lightning. Such a moment can stimulate powerful thoughts to prowl and race. Faster, wider, deeper. And that's good, because such a moment's enormous beauty should not be wasted in small thinking.

As I look down past my knees into the bouldered greenness of the cascading valley below, I have such an urge to lean forward (ever so easy) and slip from my perch; go gliding down and down and down; soaring and swooping and turning about in great glorious circles; crisp air whistles through my feathers and flexes my wingtips; my sharp eyes dart and search for some fat, juicy marmot innocently sunning on the boulders far below.

The urge is so strong, so hypnotic and compelling. I have to hug tight against the solid rock beside me. Closing my eyes to vision, holding my breath until desire releases my body and leaves me alone and shuddering — to try again some other day.

I chuckle to myself at this short craziness, but I am shaken at heart. The magic of the land can be most powerful: I wonder how many others before me have fallen prey to its siren call and dived headlong into other valleys.

A tricky, sudden little breeze teases my nose with faint vanilla perfume from the carpet of Jeffrey pines on the slopes so many thousand feet below.

Their early morning sweetness tingles along my neck and brings a flush of warmth to my face, waking me from dreams and bringing me to my feet, guiding me from my granite aerie to stride across the bald, gray outcrops and join my friends at their tents for breakfast.

Soon I breathed the good aroma of camp coffee.

How fine it is to live.

A MOUNTAIN HIGH can take your breath away.

Mountains are the beginning and the end of all natural scenery.
— *John Ruskin*

Yesterday it seems, but really last fall, I backpacked into the White Mountains with some of our museum's staff, scouting the terrain. Later we planned to take a group of young people there to study this high, desolate country.

The White Mountain range towers in Southeastern California, a bastioned Rhine-castle guarding the cattle town of Bishop, its peaks walling the east side of the Owens Valley. Besides White Mountain, at 14,200-something-or-other-feet the second-highest massif in the state, this starkly rugged range creates just about the most desolate, uninhabited, out-of-the-way place you can imagine (except, possibly, for some of the below-sea-level desert areas of Death Valley.)

These mountains aren't in the least like the nearby Sierra Nevada: lush, green, alpine meadows, sparkling mountain springs, silent groves of sky-tall trees. No, the White Mountains are just the opposite. High desert: intense, almost unbearable heat by day, and boulder-shattering freeze by night. Unless, of course, it decides to stay hot around the clock, which it often does.

The White Mountains contain the biggest mule deer with the biggest racks in the state. And bighorn sheep, wild horses and 5,000-year-old, still-living bristlecone pines.

They spread mile after mile of seemingly desolate peaks and rolling plateaus, all covered by a thick carpet of dull-green sage that exhales clouds of aromatic, sinus-clearing fumes to sear your sunburned face and protesting lungs at every exhausting step.

Water is so scarce that the few active springs have to be carefully marked on your map. (You also have to check often that they're still on the active list, or else!)

It was almost 100 degrees when we parked our van at 7,000 feet in Indian Canyon. Eleven o'clock. Sweat cascaded off our bodies and we hadn't yet shouldered our packs. Heartening indeed.

It's really difficult to acclimate yourself with a pack, at these altitudes. You gasp for each breath while your body frantically rushes to adapt itself to this startling new environment by producing more and more red blood cells to carry enough scarce oxygen from your screaming lungs. You always try to take it slowly, to give your body the time it needs. But the pizza-oven heat, and your anxiety to get on up the hill, and the steepness of the stupid trail, all combine to raise your blood pressure and give you a screaming, pounding headache. (Why did I think this was going to be fun?)

But somehow, as you plod up that narrow canyon, your head finally slows down as your body catches up. (Or maybe it's the aspirins you've been munching like peanuts.) Maybe it's the fresh, unpolluted air — real *oxygen!* It has an odor of its own. Actually, I think it's the lack of an odor that you smell. Don't ask me to explain.

Maybe it's the sudden realization that, even in this arid heat, you're up so high that it's still springtime (in September!). The "desert" around you is all adrift in reds and blues and pinks and purples that wave in the chancy breezes like an ever-surging pot of bubbling hot paints.

For sure, a difference comes with the first trickling liquid-ice spring that you find. Your body wants it so bad you can smell it. A tiny sliver of the purest ice water melts from the earth in the very center of a green patch of pungent mint, carrying with it the aromatic charge of those plants to open your head and miraculously wash away the sweat.

Our first camp is at the 9,000-foot level. Level? It's about as steep as a roof. But we do the best we can and somehow it's more than enough; our aching muscles welcome a rest at *any* level. And the view. Ah, the view!

It's been there all the while, of course, but now it taps our shoulders from behind like a friend, to fill us with wonder. We forget the rock beneath our feet; our eyes reach out to caress the bright horizons and linger on the distant mountain turrets.

But a wayward gust unthralls us, returns us to earth and our position. The sky has darkened with startling swiftness, eddies of wind earnestly pull and suck, dreadnoughts of cumulus rush in, signaling a mountain storm. A long, low rumble reaches from the distance.

As we scramble to put up our tent, an epidemic of uncontrollable grinning breaks out; the far-away rumbling gets louder, like advancing artillery strikes crashing slowly up the hill, sighting in on our position. Now we see the flashes of the giant mortars as they barrage across the unprotected valley. We brace for the attack.

FLASH! One-thousand . . . two-thousand . . . three-thouand . . . BLAM! Less than a mile away and closing. The clouds aren't very much higher than we are. It gives one a lot to think about in an electrical thunderstorm.

Abruptly, the air around us, skimpy as it is, is thick with water. An aerial flash-flood. Giant drops strip the dead needles from the pinon pines around us, and tough live needles too.

We dive under our flimsy blue nylon, and huddle. Waiting.

We aren't alone. In the violence of the storm, a gold-crowned sparrow follows us into the tent and perches quietly on a boot.

Sizzling lightning strikes out at us like a rattler's tongue. So close. The stroboscopic flash and consuming noise of the rapidly expanding gases combine to give us an instant of awareness so painfully honest as to leave us wide-eyed in astonishment.

Again . . . and again . . . AND AGAIN!

And then it's gone, moving across the valley as quickly as it came, to present an extraordinary light show against the fading pink skylines.

We didn't even see the sparrow leave.

IT'S TIME to reach for the sky.

Fall has finally come to my house.

The leaves of the trumpet vine that winds around my sliding glass doors are starting to color and dry. Though still a lush youthful green across the top, they limply fade down the sides of the doorway like an old man's gray hair. First a weak chartreuse, then dimly yellow, and finally lying brown and dried across the sill.

An earthy cascade of life to death, framing my doorway into winter.

Soon, there will be nothing there but bare dead branches. The winds will blow the leaves into dust and the rains will follow to wash the residue away. Ashes to ashes, dust to dust, and it all melts down into the earth to lie quietly waiting until it magically sprouts back again as new green leaves next spring.

The leaves are also dropping from the bushy walls around my yard to expose the birds that nightly use them for a bed. Where once I only heard sleepy peeps, I now see gray fuzzy balls perched in a line along the limb. Huddled closer than usual against the wind that is whistling in through the ever-widening cracks.

And you should see all the new visitors at my feeder, hungrily wolfing seeds. Every other day I fill it, now, just to keep up with the crowds. You'd think I was the only snack bar on the block.

Famished flocks of black-crowned sparrows in mid-migration. Tiny warblers flashing by too fast for me to key, so I shall just call them little yellow birds and be happy that I didn't blink and miss them all together. And soon I'll be hearing faint honking from lively creatures flying much too high to meet my eager eye.

Winter travelers in the middle of their long flights to the south. Stopping off to rest and eat and treat my eyes to a visual feast before fluttering on their way once more.

Even a little snail responds to the call of fall.

On the outside wall below my kitchen window, down in the snugness where grass meets wood, a snail has stuck itself against the house. Sealed tight with snaily superglue against the wet and cold, until it feels the warmth again next year.

The other night I couldn't sleep and finally rose in the wee small hours of the day. Pulling on warm pants and socks and my thick wool Pendleton sweater, I slid open the door and eased out into the chilly, cheek-tingling night and groped for the patio chair at the edge of the porch.

Crunching across the broken trumpet vine leaves in the darkness had a strangely disorienting effect on my senses. It was just as if I were walking in the woods. I felt so strongly that I was strolling across a leaf-littered forest floor that I was actually surprised that the smooth aluminum chair I touched was not a rough-barked tree trunk.

I had barely seated myself and leaned

Coldly, sadly
descends
The Autumn
evening. The field
Strewn with its dark
yellow drifts
Of withered leaves,
and the elms,
fade into dimness
apace,
Silent; hardly
a shout
From a few boys at
their play!
— Matthew Arnold.

back to stare up at the stars when I heard the quick crunch-crunch-crunch as my Siamese, Isis, followed me into the frosty fall air. Her warmth quickly filled my arms as her happy purrs wrapped around us.

It's a nice feeling — sharing such a night with a friend. There's so much to see and hear and feel. The eternal stars. A winking satellite when you know just where to look.

The faint cry of a peacock from a farm across the hill. The icy cold that gives your face and hands an extra-special aliveness.

I took in a deep breath of night and all I could smell was fireplaces.

I fell back asleep in that chair, fading away thinking one last thought.

No one should have to get up and go to work after smelling fireplaces.

OF MISTY MYSTERIES,
when fog pours down like water.

Fog has wonderful qualities.

It has swirl.

You know, like when you wade in the surf and the gray foam swirls around your legs and blows through the air in foamy bits and pieces to dance and curl around your head in sudsy little whirlwinds.

It has stealth.

I once hiked along the soft flank of a sleeping mountain as she lay soaking in a deep pool of liquid fog. I could barely see what stretched before me and was excited with each new encounter.

The sounds of my feet were lapped up by the thirsty mists and I was compelled to keep looking down to see if they were still there. It filled me with a strange sort of detached feeling, as if I were floating just above the surface of the ground. And when I would brush against a bush the sound would start and stop almost before I heard it.

A twig emerged from the silent depths, and then a branch, and then a tree. And as I stood quietly admiring it I realized, with a thrill, that a golden eagle was perched up close to the trunk. The great dark bird was busily preening and rearranging the soft white down beneath her breast feathers and I was so near I could see the blond streaks that curled down the back of her head.

I must have stood there watching for a half-hour or more. Amazed at the gentleness with which that great deadly beak straightened and combed out each tiny delicate feather.

The whole time she had her eyes closed in pleasure and secure in the protective folds of the fog; she never even saw me as I softly continued along my way.

Fog has solitude.

Years ago I spent some time on one of the Channel Islands just off the Southern California coast. One morning I awoke to discover I could not see. I sat up in my sleeping bag and there was simply nothing there but white. I was surrounded by white. Encased in white like a model in a plaster mold.

There was no sound. No gentle purring surf that last night was only 100 feet away. No crying gulls above me and from where I sat I couldn't even see the ground.

There was nothing but me as I sat buried in an avalanche of cloud.

But best of all fog has mystery.

There's something out there, you know.

Gray shadows loping along just behind you.

Common shapes turned into creative masterpieces by the artistry of an uncommon setting.

Beautiful somethings that are almost there until you look.

A sudden lonely ache from something you don't understand.

A human soul standing alone in the mist.

This world is but canvas to our imaginations.
— Thoreau (1817-1862)

Lovely! See the cloud,
the cloud appear!
Lovely! See the rain,
the rain draw near!
Who spoke?
It was the little
corn ear
High on the tip
of the stalk.
— Corn-grinding song
(Zuni)

You crouch in the rain on a ledge high in that dark freezing gully, watching the fireflies move across the valley floor as the lucky campers flee the storm. Never before have you been so cold that you can't control the violent shivering. Exhausted to the point where you can't go on, but something inside still says you do.

Once more you straddle the rope and lean back against the sopping coils to rappel down another sheer stretch of rain-oiled granite. And the friction of wet rope and clothes is so great that you barely move and nearly slip and fall into the darkness, and the adrenalin surge is just what you need to warm your cheeks and keep you going.

And your defiant shout echoes far out into that rainy night.

A sleepy, sopping sparrow huddled under a leaf in the rose bush outside my bedroom window this morning. Its eyes closed tight, its feathers fluffed against the bursts of wind, and matted by the many drops that penetrated the flimsy shelter.

It was a female gold-crowned sparrow . . . I think. I wasn't sure. All that wet had blotted out the markings.

But then a quick and violent flutter made her all warm and snug and dry again and I saw my guess was right.

Are you ever lonely?

You know, standing by a window looking out through the rainbeads at a thousand topsy outside worlds and wondering why they're so faraway kind of lonely?

It's one of the briefest of emotions. It takes just the right kind of day, a special mood, and just you.

And the most amazing thing about it is how something so infinitely fragile can swell your soul to the point of bursting and fill your eyes with tears to match the rain, without your ever knowing why.

Because just the feel of the cat against your leg, and it is gone.

Once, in the Mojave Desert, it started to rain. But it was like no rain I had ever seen before because they were giant drops, each a teaspoonful at least, and they were landing up to six feet apart.

My friend and I were amazed as we stood there listening to the loud PLOPS! as they sank into the still-hot sand and punctuated the ground around us with large wet dots.

And in a sudden moment of joyful insanity we were dashing about trying to catch one on our tongues. A mouthful of sky.

The closest I came was right between the eyes.

Nice shot, God.

RAINY DAYDREAMS bring tears to my eyes.

FALLEN VIGNETTES give new life to your breath.

You can always tell when fall arrives and summer ends.

You can feel it in your sleepy face when you open the door to share your first mug of steaming coffee with the hungry air.

My first breath swirls visibly before me like frost crystals over the lip of a hanging cornice. And my second, after a hot sip of coffee, hangs there in such a solid mass that I'm tempted to take it in my hand and shatter it loudly against the railing of my porch.

Just the thought of it, as I stand here, leaves me shivering with delight.

NIGHT

The darkness is so crystal clear that I can see the stars as plainly as if I were standing on a mountaintop.

They say that on a clear, cold night, in the utter blackness of a desert, you can see someone strike a match 10 miles or more away. As I sit here looking up into the universe, one of those mysterious lights suddenly flares briefly. And I wonder.

A dog barks far away. A sudden laugh followed by the murmur of voices. The hooting of a great horned owl. A mockingbird expounding in a brief aria. A car door slams. A house darkens.

The grass moves against my ankles, trees mutter about me, and a cool breath stirs my face.

It's as if I can hear and see and feel everything that is meant to be experienced and it is impossible to think about it all. But the physical is enough.

GEESE

Walking through a field on feet made heavy by crumbly earth, I suddenly hear the geese. Liquid musical notes falling lightly through the air beneath them like rain from V-shaped feathery clouds.

I look up to let them wet my face and soak my beard.

And I feel as if I could stand like this forever, bathed in happy voices as I watch them all fly south.

TREES

Trees are the voices of autumn.

Some speak in muted tones and share their wistful thoughts with anyone who will listen. Others let their colorful ideas float down through the air to bounce around your feet and intrude upon your thoughts.

Until the last leaf has fallen.

And then they lie there, waiting, for you to pass that way again.

I saw old Autumn in the misty morn
Stand shadowless
like silence, listening
To silence.
— Thomas Hood
(1799-1845)

House made of dawn,
House made of
evening light,
House made of the
dark cloud . . .
Dark cloud is at the
house's door,
The trail out of it is
dark cloud,
The zigzag lightning
stands high upon it.
— Night Chant
(Navajo)

SOMEWHERE BE-
HIND THE LINES —
The action is moving
closer. Bright lights lash
along eating up the ho-
rizon and the distance
rumbles like the belly of a sleeping tiger.

It's 4 a.m. and I'm crouched here on the front porch of a deserted little farmhouse near the front, scribbling in my notebook as I listen to the sounds of approaching battle. The place isn't completely deserted. There's a strange cat. Siamese. With fun-ny-looking Garfield-orange ears.

She slides between my legs and I find it pleasantly reassuring to feel her touch as we nervously watch the warring forces close in around us.

It's too warm for this time of night. Nights should always be cool. Cool so your body temperature can drop and your sleep will be deep and restful.

Hot nights mean you never get past the shallow REM state and that makes you dream and toss restlessly throughout the night.

Sometimes it means you wake up tired and uncertain in the morning.

The first round lands behind the grove of trees at the end of the block.

FLASH! BAM!

Shrapnel echoes around us.

And then a stillness that is deafening.

Her high-pitched mew is like the cry of a child and I take off my helmet and gently cover her trembling body.

And then they lay down a barrage on top of us. An endless roiling cacophony of light and sound that surges over us in

YOUR FEARLESS WAR CORRESPONDENT thunders into action.

waves and threatens to consume every last drop of our precious bodily fluids.

Lightning. Bright spears thrown by angry gods.

Often witnessed by frightened, enlight-ened, invigorated and admiring men.

And suddenly missing, hissing, awe-struck cats.

Flashback.

There was another time like this. It seems like another lifetime ago. Huddled in a tent along the ridge. Making a framework with our hands and arms out of fear that our metal tent poles might attract an errant bolt. Bodies touching in sudden need.

Struggling to keep the wind from blow-ing us out into the night. The rain from washing us down the cliffs. Our minds from driving us over the brink.

It was a joyously shattering occasion. Raising our voices in thunderous a capellá, we screamed a defiance that only the igno-rant and the unenlightened could ever share.

And then the cat came back (I thought she was a goner) and we sat and shared the slowly fading show together.

Felt the wash of rain that always follows, first in sprinkles then a rush.

Watched the first faint blush of dawn as it brightened the freshly scrubbed air.

THE LIFE 4

What is life? It is the flash of a firefly in the night. It is the breath of a buffalo in the wintertime.
— Last words of Crowfoot, a Blackfoot warrior

The real wonders in this world are simply too small to behold.

The reflections in a dewdrop.

The footprints of an ant.

A grain of crystal sand.

A single silken silver strand of web.

The web has been there for a week. A nylon rope tying a dandelion to a geranium leaf. Its 3-foot length has to measure at least a hundred yards to a spider.

My lawn needs mowing but I've waited the week out, now, waiting to see what spidery designs are in store for me next. If I mow it down, I'll never know.

I've never seen the spider but I know it's there. Subtle changes. Altered states. A single new bracing beam on the dandelion side yesterday. A quick silken wrap around the geranium stem to shore up that end this morning. It stretches sturdy against the wind. A solid force against the occasional frantic lashing about of the dandelion — rearing back against the unfamiliar restraint like a wild horse against its first halter.

How do you get inside a spider's head to see the thoughts that spark and flicker there? I don't even know if "thoughts" is the proper word. Does a spider think? Does think mean the same to an arachnid as it does to me? Does it know why it made its body weave that single string? Or does it crouch there in the crotch of a geranium trunk, waiting for an even greater calling? For the juices to stir within and remind it of its destiny?

And what of me?

SMALL IS ALL when you think like a spider.

Why has this responsibility been handed to me? Why should I care one whit what happens to it? Who or what made me the keeper of the web?

If I hadn't even seen it, hadn't caught that first silvery glint out of the corner of my eye when the sun hit it just right, would my responsibility be less? And what OF my responsibility? Is it real, or assumed?

I am no fanatic, stepping carefully to avoid the ants or wearing gauze across my mouth to keep me from breathing in and killing microscopic life. Although I cannot fault you if that is what you believe.

But yet that one thin thread of steel, created by a fragile bit of living eight-legged protoplasm, has captured my fancy as if I were a helpless fly.

It stretches over my patio's canyons like a rope across Niagara Falls, waiting for the first tentative steps of the acrobat as he clutches his balance pole and wraps his frantic toes around the humming coil and tests the ever-changing winds.

No way that thread would ever catch an insect. I touched it myself, gently. There are no sticky globules affixed to it. It is designed only to hold, a job it does incredibly well.

I press gently and the plants on both ends respond by genuflecting . . . and I stop.

Who am I to mess with this? What do I

know of spider motivations?

All I know is that every night when I get home from work, the grass has risen taller, the dandelion bows even deeper and that silver strand stretches its growing presence across my lawn.

Though my spider's slender creation is insignificant in a world where big is best, should my . . . our . . . interest be any the less?

Is the squeak of a frightened mouse any less important than the cry of the hunting eagle?

Is one giant step for mankind on the moon any greater than the twitch of a spider's abdomen in my yard?

Tell me — have you ever heard such an outlandish excuse to keep from mowing the lawn?

I thought not.

THE LAST WILD CONDOR
will fly no more.

Somewhere . . . the last wild California condor sits alone high on a rocky ledge.

The next-to-last wild California condor was captured last Friday afternoon in a final effort to save these great birds from extinction by breeding them in captivity. Of the 27 birds that are known to exist, 26 are now in captivity, 13 in a breeding colony at the San Diego Wild Animal Park, and 13 at the Los Angeles Zoo.

And in the wild, where once they did those wild condor things like picking a mate, courtship and breeding, and the raising of baby chicks on their own, there is only one wild male left.

And soon, when they catch him, there will be none.

It fills me with a great, uncertain sadness just to know this. With maybe a touch of the primal fear and infinite loneliness that must come to the last of any species that will never, ever, know a wild mate again.

Just seeing that happen to the condor should make us all pause . . . and feel.

I wonder what it would be like to be the only one of your kind that's left in the world? To a wild animal, the brothers in a cage do not exist.

How would it feel to know the only voice you will ever hear again will only be yours? Maybe only when you cry.

How would it feel to never again be able to look up and smile into the eyes of someone you know? Not even a someone you never met.

How would it feel to never be able to touch another, or to hold, or to be held?

How would it feel knowing that just the pleasure of sharing someone's company — of being there, together — will be lost to you forever?

This morning . . . somewhere, maybe even as you read this . . . that last great wild creature will spread his 10-foot wings, as he always has each day before, to warm them in the sun. All the great vultures use the ultra-violet rays to sterilize their feathers; to kill the bacteria they might have picked up when dining the night before. Mother Nature's natural way of caring for her own.

Only this time I think it will somehow be different.

He will stand like an enormous dark cross on top of the tallest rock he can find, with those stiff, hard-edged feathers curving out into a wonderous black fan with just a highlight of white shadow to give them life.

Because now he is a symbol, an obelisk, a tale once told . . . for all the rest of us who are left to see. And feel.

And then with a great shake of his wings, he will tip forward, curving his spindly white toes around the rock, and shove his heavy body into the still-crisp morning air and slip sideways across the sky like a glider tossed by some giant hand until he finds the air that's strong and brave enough to hold him up and keep him from crashing to the ground.

He will cut grand, ever-widening circles that criss-cross the sharp ridges until he finds a sunny saddle where the warm air is rising from the valley. And there he will hitch a ride on that thermal elevator, letting the heat take him and his wings high into the sky.

Up he will go, in faster, ever-tightening circles, round and round and growing smaller with each turn.

Up, and up . . .

Higher, higher . . .

Until he's just a speck in your eye.

And then he's gone.

Forever.

Some things are meant to be personal.

Some things should be kept to yourself.

Yeah.

But it's hard, because I have a friend who is contemplating suicide.

A fatal illness. Pain. Fear of becoming a vegetable. All are contributing to my friend's thoughts. Having once experienced a chronic and painfully debilitating illness myself, and having thought similar thoughts, I can see both sides. But I'm well now, and that also colors my perspective.

So I have something to say to this friend, only I don't know quite what it is, or how to say it. At least I didn't until I saw something happen last week that stimulated a rush of long-buried feelings.

The treetop outside my fourth-floor window has grown so much these last two years.

A swallowtail butterfly, pictureframed in the roomlike hollow in its topmost branches. Just level with my chest if I go out and stand on the balcony. Greenness. A green room. A natural prison.

The butterfly — I just happened to see it as I sat reading — seemed trapped there.

It caught my eyes, the moving, fluttering, yellow-black flower. Gently bouncing off the green leaves, pausing, resting to hang bobbing on the end of a twig.

I watched it, off and on, through the afternoon. Fluttering from one side of the little room to the other. Banging into leaves, butting branches, trying, always trying, but never just quite making it through.

THE WILL TO WIN is what makes us humans different.

Fly downward, idiot. I thought. There's plenty enough room to make it out. But that was from my objective viewpoint. I was not out there struggling in the green.

The next morning, when I opened the drapes and window to let in the fresh air, I saw it there. Still quietly clinging to a leaf.

When I got home, it was still there, only on another leaf. And when I leaned out and peered closely across the six-foot rift, I could see a slight fraying to the tips of both wings.

That evening it was still there, and I really began to get concerned. But how could I help? It was too high to climb and the branches would not bear my weight if I could. Frustrated, I could only watch.

The next morning it was gone. And I finally felt relief.

Two days later, while walking to my car, I passed under the tree. By my foot I caught a glimpse of black and yellow and bent down and found the dried-up husk of that gentle, ultra-light flying machine. Unable to physically push itself from its treetop prison, and unaware that it had to fly downward to escape, it had finally found the ultimate release in death.

One of the things that seems to make humans different from most other living creatures (I'm not yet ready to concede *all*), is our ability to imagine the future. To anticipate. Maybe that's the difference between calmly sitting on a leaf until you die, and hastening the process yourself.

Both are equally tragic in their own way. The loss of yet another wild and fragile creature. The loss of yet another friend.

And I can't begin to understand the right or the wrong of it, or what it all ultimately means. But that's not the purpose of this column — to quibble with the way of things. To argue with the god or gods on the why or why-nots of life.

I'd just like to advance the suggestion that a man or a woman is even more infinitely beautiful and durable than a simple little black-and-yellow butterfly.

If only because you *can* come up with that extra little effort when you find yourself struggling against the leaves.

Because we have been gifted with the sense to try.

ESCAPE with me and we'll go hug a tree.

ESCAPE

Sometimes I whisper as I walk.

Talking to myself, letting my words tumble off into nothingness in the wind. It doesn't matter. There's no one to hear but me.

How often have you walked like that? Oblivious to the what, the where and the when of it because you're all caught up in the why?

I like it best with the sweet warm breath of a dying day in my face, with the shadows long and thin and merging into night.

It has its own special calm, like a reassuring hug from a special friend or a long, satisfying kiss from someone you love.

DISCOVERY

Have you ever hugged a Jeffrey pine?

Some say the sap smells like pineapple. Personally, I say it's vanilla.

Such a question may not mean the end of the world, but it's the only thing you can think of to debate as you stand there with your arms stretched wide and your cheek pressed hard against the coarse, rutted bark in a vain attempt to be something more than just another bump on a log.

Hugging a tree has a way of putting your mind and body in close harmony with the way of all things. Try it. It's an experience you're not likely to forget. And one you'll surely want to do again each time you meet a new tree you haven't met before. (Pick your human friends wisely because not everyone may understand.)

They're all different, you know? Even those trees of the same species have their own individual personalities.

If you are a beginner, pick a large tree. One that you can't quite reach all the way around. Grab an armful and reach for the sky — look up and follow it all the way to the top with your eyes.

The first thing you will discover is that it *moves*. Maybe not a lot, depending on which way the wind blows. Maybe just an easy back and forth and back and forth. It's very disorienting and may make you feel a little bit dizzy at first. But the most amazing thing happens.

You actually *feel* the life in that tree.

You feel every creak and groan and subtle moan as the living wood strains against the constraints of the earth that gives it support.

It's as if the trunk has become living, breathing muscle.

And the tree has become your friend.

SURPRISE

The fringe-toed sand lizard has big feet.

All the better to keep it from sinking and drowning in the grainy liquid depths of the sand dunes on which it lives.

Have you ever tried running on the beach?

The infinitely fine grains of desert crystal make beach sand seem as stable as running on cement.

The fringe-toed sand lizard has adapted to this unique environment with overlapping fringes between its toes, weaving each foot into a wide curving sand-shoe. As they build up speed they raise up on their hind legs and race across the dunes with such speed that all you can see is a row of little puffs — like a quick splatter of bullets from a machine gun.

If pursued by a predator, the sand lizard will zip around a bunch of dune grass, slide to a quick stop, and with a sudden violent shiver will sink beneath the sandy surface. A few quick strokes under the sand and no trace remains of its passing.

I once spent an afternoon following those desert speedsters, hoping to capture one for a photograph.

Late in the day I followed a set of tracks around the corner of a dune until they abruptly disappeared. Smiling to myself I dropped to my knees, carefully calculated the direction of travel . . . allowed for about a foot of underground movement . . . ran my fingers lightly through the sand . . . and scooped up the sleepy coils of a napping sidewinder rattlesnake.

Oh Jeeze! Not Fair!

Amazing what extreme terror does for one's throwing reflexes.

Afterward I sat back in the sand and roared with laughter at the lizard's little joke.

RETURN

I have to go back to that other world now.

But my heart's not in it.

THE LAST LEAF fell from my tree this morning.

The last leaf fell from my tree this morning.

I remember I was standing at the kitchen sink, drinking my first cup of coffee and looking out the window at the fog.

Have you ever really looked at the fog? It's not really the fog you're looking at, you know. It's what you're looking at through it.

Fog is an artist and it lets you look at things with someone else's eyes. Someone mysterious and moody, who dresses in billowy gray robes.

That's when I saw the leaf fall.

I remember thinking it was as if the fog had plucked it from the branch and then dropped it into a gray-lined pocket.

It was very early and I was the only one up. I often rise early, to allow myself the pleasures of that quiet time. That moment of aloneness when one can identify with one's self.

You see, those leaves had been falling daily for weeks. And I'd rake and rake and rake, and pause for breath, or go into the house to answer the phone, and when I returned, many more had fallen.

It was as if the tree had leaves that fell forever.

And now, incredibly, I was on hand to witness the downfall of the ultimate leaf.

The last of its kind. The end of a race that is born, achieves greatness, and then dies — all in a single year.

I caught myself wondering — what if I hadn't been there to see? Would it have been the same?

I finally think I understand.

WHAT IS LIFE?
Is it hate? Is it love?

What is life?

Is it all those nice things you want but never seem to find?

Is it something you can buy in a store? Or is it something you know, but just can't put into words?

Is it the happiness and the sadness, and all those other big and little ups and downs, and all the heavy tones and pastel shades of different feelings in between?

Is it the ache of your loneliness, like when you're staring through the pane into that early morning darkness, caught up in the cold grip of the kitchen, praying that the first cup of coffee will set you free?

Is it fear? Like when you're very sick and afraid to die? Or when you finally think you're old? Or feel you are no longer handsome, or pretty? Or something unexplained that you don't understand, except that you know it's there and don't know why? Or maybe something simple, like the big mean dog that lives down the block, or having to stand up and say something meaningful to a large group of people?

Is it freedom? The knowledge that you can do things because you want to, or help someone because you care, or accept something because you need, or just be you because you are?

Or is it a lack of freedom? Of going to work each day and doing something you hate, of being something that you aren't, of wanting something you can't have, of needing something you can't seem to find, of not knowing who you really are?

Is it taking a walk through an alpine meadow, and feeling yourself sink through first the soft green moss and then the chocolate mud until the icy mountain water soaks through your boots and cools your feet? And liking it? Or hating it?

Is it tripping on a rug, or pouring coffee in your lap, or someone else's, or getting caught picking your nose, or staring when you shouldn't, or otherwise exploring one of the thousand and one ways that exist only for you to make a fool of yourself?

Is it hate? The unexplained blackness in us all that lurks and prowls inside our heads, just waiting for the cage to be unlocked, to let the beast sneak out and feed?

Is it love? That unexplainable something that sometimes fills your whole infinite self to the point where it is best expressed by just standing together and holding each other and feeling yourselves burst into oneness?

Is it being loved? And knowing?

Is it everything you know, and all those things you've yet to learn, and every feeling that you've ever felt and have yet to feel, and whatever else there is that's left to be discovered?

Is life something to be desired, no matter what the day may bring, or what comes out at night?

Oh yes!

. . . if one advances confidently in the direction of his dreams, and endeavors to live the life which he has imagined, he will meet with a success unexpected in common hours.
— Thoreau (Walden, "Conclusion")

123